Great Britain at War

Jeffery Farnol

GREAT BRITAIN
AT WAR

BY

JEFFERY FARNOL

1918

BY JEFFERY FARNOL

THE BROAD HIGHWAY
THE AMATEUR GENTLEMAN
THE HONOURABLE MR. TAWNISH
BELTANE THE SMITH
THE DEFINITE OBJECT

To

ALL MY

AMERICAN FRIENDS

CONTENTS

I

FOREWORD

In publishing these collected articles in book form (the result of my visits to Flanders, the battlefields of France and divers of the great munition centres), some of which have already appeared in the press both in England and America, I do so with a certain amount of diffidence, because of their so many imperfections and of their inadequacy of expression. But what man, especially in these days, may hope to treat a theme so vast, a tragedy so awful, without a sure knowledge that all he can say must fall so infinitely far below the daily happenings which are, on the one hand, raising Humanity to a godlike altitude or depressing it lower than the brutes. But, because these articles are a simple record of what I have seen and what I have heard, they may perhaps be of use in bringing out of the shadow— that awful shadow of "usualness" into which they have fallen— many incidents that would, before the war, have roused the world to wonder, to pity and to infinite awe.

Since the greater number of these articles was written, America has thrown her might into the scale against merciless Barbarism and Autocracy; at her entry into the drama there was joy in English and French hearts, but, I venture to think, a much greater joy in the hearts of all true Americans. I happened to be in Paris on the memorable day America declared war, and I shall never forget the deep-souled enthusiasm of the many Americans it was my privilege to know there. America, the greatest democracy in the world, had at last taken her stand on the side of Freedom, Justice and Humanity.

As an Englishman, I love and am proud of my country, and, in the years I spent in America, I saw with pain and deep regret the misunderstanding that existed between these two great nations. In America I beheld a people young, ardent, indomitable, full of the unconquerable spirit of Youth, and I thought of that older country across the seas, so little understanding and so little understood.

And often I thought if it were only possible to work a miracle, if it were only possible for the mists of jealousy and ill-feeling, or rivalry and misconception to be swept away once and for all—if only these

1

two great nations could be bonded together by a common ideal, heart to heart and hand to hand, for the good of Humanity, what earthly power should ever be able to withstand their united strength. In my soul I knew that the false teaching of history—that great obstacle to the progress of the world—was one of the underlying causes of the misunderstanding, but it was an American Ambassador who put this into words. If, said he, America did not understand the aims and hopes of Great Britain, *it was due to the textbooks of history used in American schools.*

To-day, America, through her fighting youth and manhood, will see Englishmen as they are, and not as they have been represented. Surely the time has come when we should try and appreciate each other at our true worth.

These are tragic times, sorrowful times, yet great and noble times, for these are days of fiery ordeal whereby mean and petty things are forgotten and the dross of unworthy things burned away. To-day the two great Anglo-Saxon peoples stand united in a noble comradeship for the good of the world and for those generations that are yet to be, a comradeship which I, for one, do most sincerely hope and pray may develop into a veritable brotherhood. One in blood are we, in speech, and in ideals, and though sundered by generations of misunderstanding and false teaching, to-day we stand, brothers-in-arms, fronting the brute for the freedom of Humanity.

Americans will die as Britons have died for this noble cause; Americans will bleed as Britons have bled; American women will mourn as British women have mourned these last terrible years; yet, in these deaths, in this noble blood, in these tears of agony and bereavement, surely the souls of these two great nations will draw near, each to each, and understand at last.

Here in a word is the fulfilment of the dream; that, by the united effort, by the blood, by the suffering, by the heartbreak endured of these two great English-speaking races, wars shall be made to cease in all the world; that peace and happiness, truth and justice shall be established among us for all generations, and that the united powers of the Anglo-Saxon races shall be a bulwark behind which Mankind may henceforth rest secure.

Now, in the name of Humanity, I appeal to American and to Briton to work for, strive, think and pray for this great and glorious consummation.

II
CARTRIDGES

At an uncomfortable hour I arrived at a certain bleak railway platform and in due season, stepping into a train, was whirled away northwards. And as I journeyed, hearkening to the talk of my companions, men much travelled and of many nationalities, my mind was agog for the marvels and wonders I was to see in the workshops of Great Britain. Marvels and wonders I was prepared for, and yet for once how far short of fact were all my fancies!

Britain has done great things in the past; she will, I pray, do even greater in the future; but surely never have mortal eyes looked on an effort so stupendous and determined as she is sustaining, and will sustain, until this most bloody of wars is ended.

The deathless glory of our troops, their blood and agony and scorn of death have been made pegs on which to hang much indifferent writing and more bad verse—there have been letters also, sheaves of them, in many of which effusions one may discover a wondering surprise that our men can actually and really fight, that Britain is still the Britain of Drake and Frobisher and Grenville, of Nelson and Blake and Cochrane, and that the same deathless spirit of heroic determination animates her still.

To-night, as I pen these lines, our armies are locked in desperate battle, our guns are thundering on many fronts, but like an echo to their roar, from mile upon mile of workshops and factories and shipyards is rising the answering roar of machinery, the thunderous crash of titanic hammers, the hellish rattle of riveters, the whining, droning, shrieking of a myriad wheels where another vast army is engaged night and day, as indomitable, as fierce of purpose as the army beyond the narrow seas.

I have beheld miles of workshops that stand where grass grew two short years ago, wherein are bright-eyed English girls, Irish colleens and Scots lassies by the ten thousand, whose dexterous fingers flash nimbly to and fro, slender fingers, yet fingers contriving death. I have wandered through a wilderness of whirring driving-belts and humming wheels where men and women, with the same feverish activity, bend above machines whose very hum sang to me of death, while I have watched a cartridge grow from a disc of metal to the hellish contrivance it is.

And as I watched the busy scene it seemed an unnatural and awful thing that women's hands should be busied thus, fashioning means for the maiming and destruction of life—until, in a remote corner, I paused to watch a woman whose dexterous fingers were fitting finished cartridges into clips with wonderful celerity. A middle-aged woman, this, tall and white-haired, who, at my remark, looked up with a bright smile, but with eyes sombre and weary.

"Yes, sir," she answered above the roar of machinery, "I had two boys at the front, but—they're a-laying out there somewhere, killed by the same shell. I've got a photo of their graves—very neat they look, though bare, and I'll never be able to go and tend 'em, y'see— nor lay a few flowers on 'em. So I'm doin' this instead—to help the other lads. Yes, sir, my boys did their bit, and now they're gone their mother's tryin' to do hers."

Thus I stood and talked with this sad-eyed, white-haired woman who had cast off selfish grief to aid the Empire, and in her I saluted the spirit of noble motherhood ere I turned and went my way.

But now I woke to the fact that my companions had vanished utterly; lost, but nothing abashed, I rambled on between long alleys of clattering machines, which in their many functions seemed in themselves almost human, pausing now and then to watch and wonder and exchange a word with one or other of the many workers, until a kindly works-manager found me and led me unerringly through that riotous jungle of machinery.

He brought me by devious ways to a place he called "holy ground"—long, low outbuildings approached by narrow, wooden causeways, swept and re-swept by men shod in felt—a place this, where no dust or grit might be, for here was the magazine, with the filling sheds beyond. And within these long sheds, each seated behind a screen, were women who handled and cut deadly cordite into needful lengths as if it had been so much ribbon, and always and everywhere the same dexterous speed.

He led me, this soft-voiced, keen-eyed works-manager, through well-fitted wards and dispensaries, redolent of clean, druggy smells and the pervading odour of iodoform; he ushered me through dining halls long and wide and lofty and lighted by many windows, where countless dinners were served at a trifling cost per head; and so at last out upon a pleasant green, beyond which rose the great gates where stood the cars that were to bear my companions and myself upon our way.

"They seem to work very hard!" said I, turning to glance back whence we had come, "they seem very much in earnest."

"Yes," said my companion, "every week we are turning out—" here he named very many millions—"of cartridges."

"To be sure they are earning good money!" said I thoughtfully.

"More than many of them ever dreamed of earning," answered the works-manager. "And yet—I don't know, but I don't think it is altogether the money, somehow."

"I'm glad to hear you say that—very glad!" said I, "because it is a great thing to feel that they are working for the Britain that is, and is to be."

III
RIFLES AND LEWIS GUNS

A drive through a stately street where were shops which might rival Bond Street, the Rue de la Paix, or Fifth Avenue for the richness and variety of their contents; a street whose pavements were thronged with well-dressed pedestrians and whose roadway was filled with motor cars—vehicles, these, scornful of the petrol tax and such-like mundane and vulgar restrictions—in fine, the street of a rich and thriving city.

But suddenly the stately thoroughfare had given place to a meaner street, its princely shops had degenerated into blank walls or grimy yards, on either hand rose tall chimney stacks belching smoke; instead of dashing motor cars, heavy wains and cumbrous wagons jogged by; in place of the well-dressed throng were figures rough-clad and grimy that hurried along the narrow sidewalks—but these rough-clad people walked fast and purposefully. So we hummed along streets wide or narrow but always grimy, until we were halted at a tall barrier by divers policemen, who, having inspected our credentials, permitted us to pass on to the factory, or series of factories, that stretched themselves before us, building on building— block on block—a very town.

Here we were introduced to various managers and heads of departments, among whom was one in the uniform of a Captain of Engineers, under whose capable wing I had the good fortune to come, for he, it seemed, had lived among engines and machinery, had thought out and contrived lethal weapons from his youth up, and therewith retained so kindly and genial a personality as drew me irresistibly. Wherefore I gave myself to his guidance, and he, chatting of books and literature and the like trivialities, led me along corridors and passage-ways to see the wonder of the guns. And as we went, in the air about us was a stir, a hum that grew and ever grew, until, passing a massive swing door, there burst upon us a rumble, a roar, a clashing din.

We stood in a place of gloom lit by many fires, a vast place whose roof was hid by blue vapour; all about us rose the dim forms of huge stamps, whose thunderous stroke beat out a deep diapason to the ring of countless hand-hammers. And, lighted by the sudden glare of furnace fires were figures, bare-armed, smoke-grimed, wild of aspect, figures that whirled heavy sledges or worked the levers of the giant steam-hammers, while here and there bars of iron new-glowing from the furnace winked and twinkled in the gloom where those wild, half-naked men-shapes flitted to and fro unheard amid the thunderous din. Awed and half stunned, I stood viewing that never-to-be-forgotten scene until I grew aware that the Captain was roaring in my ear.

"Forge ... rifle barrels ... come and see and mind where you tread!"

Treading as seemingly silent as those wild human shapes, that straightened brawny backs to view me as I passed, that grinned in the fire-glow and spoke one to another, words lost to my stunned hearing, ere they bent to their labour again, obediently I followed the Captain's dim form until I was come where, bare-armed, leathern-aproned and be-spectacled, stood one who seemed of some account among these salamanders, who, nodding to certain words addressed to him by the Captain, seized a pair of tongs, swung open a furnace door, and plucking thence a glowing brand, whirled it with practised ease, and setting it upon the dies beneath a huge steam-hammer, nodded his head. Instantly that mighty engine fell to work, thumping and banging with mighty strokes, and with each stroke that glowing steel bar changed and changed, grew round, grew thin, hunched a shoulder here, showed a flat there, until, lo! before my eyes was the shape of a rifle minus the stock! Hereupon the be-spectacled salamander nodded again, the giant hammer became immediately immobile, the glowing forging was set among hundreds of others and a voice roared in my ear:

"Two minutes ... this way."

A door opens, closes, and we are in sunshine again, and the Captain is smilingly reminiscent of books.

"This is greater than books," said I.

"Why, that depends," says he, "there are books and books ... this way!"

Up a flight of stairs, through a doorway, and I am in a shop where huge machines grow small in perspective. And here I see the rough forging pass through the many stages of trimming, milling, turning, boring, rifling until comes the assembling, and I take up the finished rifle ready for its final process—testing. So downstairs we go to the testing sheds, wherefrom as we approach comes the sound of dire battle, continuous reports, now in volleys, now in single sniping shots, or in rapid succession.

Inside, I breathe an air charged with burnt powder and behold in a long row, many rifles mounted upon crutches, their muzzles levelled at so many targets. Beside each rifle stand two men, one to sight and correct, and one to fire and watch the effect of the shot by means of a telescope fixed to hand.

With the nearest of these men I incontinent fell into talk—a chatty fellow this, who, busied with pliers adjusting the back-sight of a rifle, talked to me of lines of sight and angles of deflection, his remarks sharply punctuated by rifle-shots, that came now slowly, now in twos and threes and now in rapid volleys.

"Yes, sir," said he, busy pliers never still, "guns and rifles is very like us—you and me, say. Some is just naturally good and some is worse than bad—load up, George! A new rifle's like a kid—pretty sure to fire a bit wide at first—not being used to it—we was all kids once, sir, remember! But a bit of correction here an' there'll put that right as a rule. On the other hand there's rifles as Old Nick himself nor nobody else could make shoot straight—ready, George? And it's just the same with kids! Now, if you'll stick your eyes to that glass, and watch the target, you'll see how near she'll come this time—all right, George!" As he speaks the rifle speaks also, and observing the hit on the target, I sing out:

"Three o'clock!"

Ensues more work with the pliers; George loads and fires and with one eye still at the telescope I give him:

"Five o'clock!"

Another moment of adjusting, again the rifle cracks and this time I announce:

"A bull!"

Hereupon my companion squints through the glass and nods: "Right-oh, George!" says he, then, while George the silent stacks the tested rifle with many others, he turns to me and nods, "Got 'im that time, sir—pity it weren't a bloomin' Hun!"

Here the patient Captain suggests we had better go, and unwillingly I follow him out into the open and the sounds of battle die away behind us.

And now, as we walked, I learned some particulars of that terrible device the Lewis gun; how that it could spout bullets at the rate of six hundred per minute; how, by varying pressures of the trigger, it could be fired by single rounds or pour forth its entire magazine in a continuous, shattering volley and how it weighed no more than twenty-six pounds.

"And here," said the Captain, opening a door and speaking in his pleasant voice, much as though he were showing me some rare flowers, "here is where they grow by the hundred, every week."

And truly in hundreds they were, long rows of them standing very neatly in racks, their walnut stocks heel by heel, their grim, blue muzzles in long, serried ranks, very orderly and precise; and something in their very orderliness endowed them with a certain individuality as it were. It almost seemed to me that they were waiting, mustered and ready, for that hour of ferocious roar and tumult when their voice should be the voice of swift and terrible death. Now as I gazed upon them, filled with these scarcely definable thoughts, I was startled by a sudden shattering crash near by, a sound made up of many individual reports, and swinging about, I espied a man seated upon a stool; a plump, middle-aged, family sort of man, who sat upon his low stool, his aproned knees set wide, as plump, middle-aged family men often do. As I watched, Paterfamilias squinted along the sights of one of these guns and once again came that shivering crash that is like nothing else I ever heard. Him I approached and humbly ventured an awed question or so, whereon he graciously beckoned me nearer, vacated his stool, and motioning me to sit there, suggested I might try a shot at the target, a far disc lighted by shaded electric bulbs.

"She's fixed dead on!" he said, "and she's true—you can't miss. A quick pull for single shots and a steady pressure for a volley."

Hereupon I pressed the trigger, the gun stirred gently in its clamps, the air throbbed, and a stream of ten bullets (the testing number) plunged into the bull's-eye and all in the space of a moment.

"There ain't a un'oly 'un of 'em all could say 'Hoch the Kaiser' with them in his stomach," said Paterfamilias thoughtfully, laying a hand upon the respectable stomach beneath his apron, "it's a gun, that is!" And a gun it most assuredly is.

I would have tarried longer with Paterfamilias, for in his own way, he was as arresting as this terrible weapon—or nearly so—but the Captain, gentle-voiced and serene as ever, suggested that my companions had a train to catch, wherefore I reluctantly turned away. But as I went, needs must I glance back at Paterfamilias, as comfortable as ever where he sat, but with pudgy fingers on trigger grimly at work again, and from him to the long, orderly rows of guns mustered in their orderly ranks, awaiting their hour.

We walked through shops where belts and pulleys and wheels and cogs flapped and whirled and ground in ceaseless concert, shops where files rasped and hammers rang, shops again where all seemed riot and confusion at the first glance, but at a second showed itself ordered confusion, as it were. And as we went, my Captain spoke of the hospital bay, of wards and dispensary (lately enlarged), of sister and nurses and the grand work they were doing among the employees other than attending to their bodily ills; and talking thus, he brought me to the place, a place of exquisite order and tidiness, yet where nurses, blue-uniformed, in their white caps, cuffs and aprons, seemed to me the neatest of all. And here I was introduced to Sister, capable, strong, gentle-eyed, who told me something of her work—how many came to her with wounds of soul as well as body;

of griefs endured and wrongs suffered by reason of pitiful lack of knowledge; of how she was teaching them care and cleanliness of minds as well as bodies, which is surely the most blessed heritage the unborn generations may inherit. She told me of the patient bravery of the women, the chivalry of grimy men, whose hurts may wait that others may be treated first. So she talked and I listened until, perceiving the Captain somewhat ostentatiously consulting his watch, I presently left that quiet haven with its soft-treading ministering attendants.

So we had tea and cigarettes, and when I eventually shook hands with my Captain, I felt that I was parting with a friend.

"And what struck you most particularly this afternoon?" enquired one of my companions.

"Well," said I, "it was either the Lewis gun or Paterfamilias the grim."

IV
CLYDEBANK

Henceforth the word "Clydebank" will be associated in my mind with the ceaseless ring and din of riveting-hammers, where, day by day, hour by hour, a new fleet is growing, destroyers and torpedo boats alongside monstrous submarines—yonder looms the grim bulk of Super-dreadnought or battle cruiser or the slender shape of some huge liner.

And with these vast shapes about me, what wonder that I stood awed and silent at the stupendous sight. But, to my companion, a shortish, thick-set man, with a masterful air and a bowler hat very much over one eye, these marvels were an everyday affair; and now, ducking under a steel hawser, he led me on, dodging moving trucks, stepping unconcernedly across the buffers of puffing engines, past titanic cranes that swung giant arms high in the air; on we went, stepping over chain cables, wire ropes, pulley-blocks and a thousand and one other obstructions, on which I stumbled occasionally since my awed gaze was turned upwards. And as we walked amid these awesome shapes, he talked, I remember, of such futile things as— books.

I beheld great ships well-nigh ready for launching; I stared up at huge structures towering aloft, a wild complexity of steel joists and girders, yet, in whose seeming confusion, the eye could detect something of the mighty shape of the leviathan that was to be; even as I looked, six feet or so of steel plating swung through the air, sank into place, and immediately I was deafened by the hellish racket of the riveting-hammers.

"... nothing like a good book and a pipe to go with it!" said my companion between two bursts of hammering.

"This is a huge ship!" said I, staring upward still.

"H'm—fairish!" nodded my companion, scratching his square jaw and letting his knowledgeful eyes rove to and fro over the vast bulk that loomed above us.

"Have you built them much bigger, then?" I enquired.

My companion nodded and proceeded to tell me certain amazing facts which the riotous riveting-hammers promptly censored in the following remarkable fashion.

"You should have seen the rat-tat-tat. We built her in exactly nineteen months instead of two years and a half! Biggest battleship afloat—two hundred feet longer than the rat-tat-tat—launched her last rat-tat-tat—gone to rat-tat-tat-tat for her guns."

"What size guns?" I shouted above the hammers.

"Rat-tat-tat-tat-tat-inch!" he said, smiling grimly.

"How much?" I yelled.

"She has four rat-tat-tat-tat inch and twelve rattle-tattle inch besides rat-tat-tat-tat!" he answered, nodding.

"Really!" I roared, "if those guns are half as big as I think, the Germans—"

"The Germans—!" said he, and blew his nose.

"How long did you say she was?" I hastened to ask as the hammers died down a little.

"Well, over all she measured exactly rat-tat feet. She was so big that we had to pull down a corner of the building there, as you can see."

"And what's her name?"

"The rat-tat-tat, and she's the rattle-tattle of her class."

"Are these hammers always quite so noisy, do you suppose?" I enquired, a little hopelessly.

"Oh, off and on!" he nodded. "Kick up a bit of a racket, don't they, but you get used to it in time; I could hear a pin drop. Look! since we've stood here they've got four more plates fixed—there goes the fifth. This way!"

Past the towering bows of future battleships he led me, over and under more steel cables, until he paused to point towards an empty slip near by.

"That's where we built the *Lusitania*!" said he. "We thought she was pretty big then—but now—!" he settled his hat a little further over one eye with a knock on the crown.

"Poor old *Lusitania*!" said I, "she'll never be forgotten."

"Not while ships sail!" he answered, squaring his square jaw, "no, she'll never be forgotten, nor the murderers who ended her!"

"And they've struck a medal in commemoration," said I.

"Medal!" said he, and blew his nose louder than before. "I fancy they'll wish they could swallow that damn medal, one day. Poor old *Lusitania*! You lose any one aboard?"

"I had some American friends aboard, but they escaped, thank God—others weren't so fortunate."

"No," he answered, turning away, "but America got quite angry—wrote a note, remember? Over there's one of the latest submarines. Germany can't touch her for speed and size, and better than that, she's got rat-tat—"

"I beg pardon?" I wailed, for the hammers were riotous again, "what has she?"

"She's got rat-tat forward and rat-tat aft, surface speed rat-tat-tat knots, submerged rat-tat-tat, and then best of all she's rattle-tattle-tattle. Yes, hammers are a bit noisy! This way. A destroyer yonder—new class—rat-tat feet longer than ordinary. We expect her to do rat-tat-tat knots and she'll mount rat-tat guns. There are two of them in the basin yonder having their engines fitted, turbines to give rat-tat-tat horse power. But come on, we'd better be going or we shall lose the others of your party."

"I should like to stay here a week," said I, tripping over a steel hawser.

"Say a month," he added, steadying me deftly. "You might begin to see all we've been doing in a month. We've built twenty-nine ships of different classes since the war began in this one yard, and we're going on building till the war's over—and after that too. And this place is only one of many. Which reminds me you're to go to another yard this afternoon—we'd better hurry after the rest of your party or they'll be waiting for you."

"I'm afraid they generally are!" I sighed, as I turned and followed my conductor through yawning doorways (built to admit a giant, it seemed) into vast workshops whose lofty roofs were lost in haze. Here I saw huge turbines and engines of monstrous shape in course of construction; I beheld mighty propellers, with boilers and furnaces big as houses, whose proportions were eloquent of the colossal ships that were to be. But here indeed, all things were on a gigantic scale; ponderous lathes were turning, mighty planing machines swung unceasing back and forth, while other monsters bored and cut through steel plate as it had been so much cardboard.

"Good machines, these!" said my companion, patting one of these monsters with familiar hand, "all made in Britain!"

"Like the men!" I suggested.

"The men," said he. "Humph! They haven't been giving much trouble lately—touch wood!"

"Perhaps they know Britain just now needs every man that is a man," I suggested, "and some one has said that a man can fight as hard at home here with a hammer as in France with a rifle."

"Well, there's a lot of fighting going on here," nodded my companion, "we're fighting night and day and we're fighting damned hard. And now we'd better hurry; your party will be cursing you in chorus."

"I'm afraid it has before now!" said I.

So we hurried on, past shops whence came the roar of machinery, past great basins wherein floated destroyers and torpedo boats, past craft of many kinds and fashions, ships built and building; on I hastened, tripping over more cables, dodging from the buffers of snorting engines and deafened again by the fearsome din of the riveting-hammers, until I found my travelling companions assembled and ready to depart. Scrambling hastily into the nearest motor car I shook hands with this shortish, broad-shouldered, square-jawed man and bared my head, for, so far as these great works were concerned, he was in very truth a superman. Thus I left him to oversee the building of these mighty ships, which have been and will ever be the might of these small islands.

But, even as I went speeding through dark streets, in my ears, rising high above the hum of our engine was the unceasing din, the remorseless ring and clash of the riveting-hammers.

V

SHIPS IN MAKING

Build me straight, O worthy Master!
   Staunch and strong, a goodly vessel,
That shall laugh at all disaster
   And with wave and whirlwind wrestle!
     —*Longfellow.*

He was an old man with that indefinable courtliness of bearing that is of a past generation; tall and spare he was, his white head bowed a little by weight of years, but almost with my first glance I seemed to recognise him instinctively for that "worthy Master Builder of goodly vessels staunch and strong!" So the Master Builder I will call him.

He stood beside me at the window with one in the uniform of a naval captain, and we looked, all three of us, at that which few might behold unmoved.

"She's a beauty!" said the Captain. "She's all speed and grace from cutwater to sternpost."

"I've been building ships for sixty-odd years and we never launched a better!" said the Master Builder.

As for me I was dumb.

She lay within a stone's throw, a mighty vessel, huge of beam and length, her superstructure towering proudly aloft, her massive armoured sides sweeping up in noble curves, a Super-Dreadnought complete from trucks to keelson. Yacht-like she sat the water all buoyant grace from lofty prow to tapering counter, and to me there was something sublime in the grim and latent power, the strength and beauty of her.

"But she's not so very—big, is she?" enquired a voice behind me.

The Captain stared; the Master Builder smiled.

"Fairly!" he nodded. "Why do you ask?"

"Well, I usually reckon the size of a ship from the number of her funnels, and—"

"Ha!" exclaimed the Captain explosively.

"Humph!" said the Master Builder gently. "After luncheon you shall measure her if you like, but now I think we will go and eat."

During a most excellent luncheon the talk ranged from ships and books and guns to submarines and seaplanes, with stories of battle and sudden death, tales of risk and hardship, of noble courage and heroic deeds, so that I almost forgot to eat and was sorry when at last we rose from table.

Once outside I had the good fortune to find myself between the Captain and the venerable figure of the Master Builder, in whose company I spent a never-to-be-forgotten afternoon. With them I stood alongside this noble ship which, seen thus near, seemed mightier than ever.

"Will she be fast?" I enquired.

"Very fast—for a Dreadnought!" said the Captain.

"And at top speed she'll show no bow wave to speak of," added the veteran. "See how fine her lines are fore and aft."

"And her gun power will be enormous!" said the Captain.

Hard by I espied a solitary being, who stood, chin in hand, lost in contemplation of this large vessel.

"Funnels or not, she's bigger than you thought?" I enquired of him.

He glanced at me, shook his head, sighed, and took himself by the chin again.

"Holy smoke!" said he.

"And you have been building ships for sixty years?" I asked of the venerable figure beside me.

"And more!" he answered; "and my father built ships hereabouts so long ago as 1820, and his grandfather before him."

"Back to the times of Nelson and Rodney and Anson," said I, "great seamen all, who fought great ships! What would they think of this one, I wonder?"

"That she was a worthy successor," replied the Master Builder, letting his eyes, so old and wise in ships, wander up and over the mighty fabric before us. "Yes," he nodded decisively, "she's worthy—like the men who will fight her one of these days."

"But our enemies and some of our friends rather thought we had degenerated these latter days," I suggested.

"Ah, well!" said he very quietly, "they know better now, don't you think?"

"Yes," said I, and again, "Yes."

"Slow starters always," continued he musingly; "but the nation that can match us in staying power has yet to be born!"

So walking between these two I listened and looked and asked questions, and of what I heard, and of what I saw I could write much; but for the censor I might tell of armour-belts of enormous thickness, of guns of stupendous calibre, of new methods of defence against sneaking submarine and torpedo attack, and of devices new and strange; but of these I may neither write nor speak, because of the aforesaid censor. Suffice it that as the sun sank, we came, all three, to a jetty whereto a steamboat lay moored, on whose limited deck were numerous figures, divers of whom beckoned me on.

So with hearty farewells, I stepped aboard the steamboat, whereupon she snorted and fell suddenly a-quiver as she nosed out into the broad stream while I stood to wave my hat in farewell.

Side by side they stood, the Captain tall and broad and sailor-like in his blue and gold—a man of action, bold of eye, hearty of voice, free of gesture; the other, his silver hair agleam in the setting sun, a man wise with years, gentle and calm-eyed, my Master Builder. Thus, as the distance lengthened, I stood watching until presently they turned, side by side, and so were gone.

Slowly we steamed down the river, a drab, unlovely waterway, but a wonderful river none the less, whose banks teem with workers where ships are building—ships by the mile, by the league; ships of all shapes and of all sizes, ships of all sorts and for many different purposes. Here are great cargo boats growing hour by hour with liners great and small; here I saw mile on mile of battleships, cruisers, destroyers and submarines of strange design with torpedo boats of uncanny shape; tramp steamers, windjammers, squat colliers and squatter tugs, these last surely the ugliest craft that ever wallowed in water. Mine layers were here with mine sweepers and hospital ships—a heterogeneous collection of well-nigh every kind of ship that floats.

Some lay finished and ready for launching, others, just begun, were only a sketch—a hint of what soon would be a ship.

On our right were ships, on our left were ships and more ships, a long perspective; ships by the million tons—until my eyes grew a-weary of ships and I went below.

Truly a wonderful river, this, surely in its way the most wonderful river eyes may see, a sight I shall never forget, a sight I shall always associate with the stalwart figure of the Captain and the white hair and venerable form of the Master Builder as they stood side by side to wave adieu.

VI
THE BATTLE CRUISERS

Beneath the shadow of a mighty bridge I stepped into a very smart launch manned by sailors in overalls somewhat grimy, and, rising and falling to the surge of the broad river, we held away for a destroyer that lay grey and phantom-like, low, rakish, and with speed in every line of her. As we drew near, her narrow deck looked to my untutored eye a confused litter of guns, torpedo tubes, guy ropes, cables and windlasses. Howbeit, I clambered aboard, and ducking under a guy rope and avoiding sundry other obstructions, shook hands with her commander, young, clear-eyed and cheery of mien, who presently led me past a stumpy smokestack and up a perpendicular ladder to the bridge where, beneath a somewhat flimsy-looking structure, was the wheel, brass-bound and highly be-polished like all else about this crowded craft as, notably, the binnacle and certain brass-bound dials, on the faces whereof one might read such words as: Ahead, Astern, Fast, Slow, etc. Forward of this was a platform, none too roomy, where was a gun most carefully wrapped and swaddled in divers cloths, tarpaulins, etc.— wrapped up with as much tender care as if it had been a baby, and delicate at that. But, as the commander casually informed me, they had been out patrolling all night and "it had blown a little"— wherefore I surmised the cloths and tarpaulins aforesaid.

"I should think," I ventured, observing her sharp lines and slender build, "I should think she would roll rather frightfully when it does blow a little?"

"Well, she does a bit," he admitted, "but not so much—Starboard!" said he, over his shoulder, to the bearded mariner at the wheel. "Take us round by the *Tiger*."

"Aye, aye, sir!" retorted the bearded one as we began to slide through the water.

"Yes, she's apt to roll a bit, perhaps, but she's not so bad," he continued; "besides, you get used to it."

Here he fell to scanning the haze ahead through a pair of binoculars, a haze through which, as we gathered speed, ghostly shapes began to loom, portentous shapes that grew and grew upon the sight, turret, superstructure and embattled mast; here a mighty battle cruiser, yonder a super-destroyer, one after another, quiet-seeming on this autumn morning, and yet whose grim hulks held latent potentialities of destruction and death, as many of them have proved but lately.

As we passed those silent, monstrous shapes, the Commander named them in turn, names which had been flashed round the earth not so long ago, names which shall yet figure in the histories to come with Grenville's *Revenge*, Drake's *Golden Hind*, Blake's *Triumph*, Anson's *Centurion*, Nelson's *Victory* and a score of other deathless names—glorious names that make one proud to be of the race that manned and fought them.

Peacefully they rode at their moorings, the water lapping gently at their steel sides, but, as we steamed past, on more than one of them, and especially the grim *Tiger*, I saw the marks of the Jutland battle in dinted plate, scarred funnel and superstructure, taken when for hours on end the dauntless six withstood the might of the German fleet.

So, as we advanced past these battle-scarred ships, I felt a sense of awe, that indefinable uplift of soul one is conscious of when treading with soft and reverent foot the dim aisles of some cathedral hallowed by time and the dust of our noble dead.

"This afternoon," said the Commander, offering me his cigarette case, "they're going to show you over the *Warspite*—the German Navy have sunk her so repeatedly, you know. There," he continued, nodding towards a fleet of squat-looking vessels with stumpy masts, "those are the auxiliaries—coal and oil and that sort of thing—ugly beggars, but useful. How about a whisky and soda?"

Following him down the perpendicular ladder, he brought me aft to a hole in the deck, a small hole, a round hole into which he proceeded to insert himself, first his long legs, then his broad shoulders, evidently by an artifice learned of much practice. Finally his jauntily be-capped head vanished, and thereafter from the deeps below his cheery voice reached me.

"I have whisky, sherry and rum—mind your head and take your choice!"

I descended into a narrow chamber divided by a longish table and flanked by berths with a chest of drawers beneath each. At the further end of this somewhat small and dim apartment and northeasterly of the table was a small be-polished stove wherein a fire burned; in a rack against a bulkhead were some half-dozen rifles, above our head was a rack for cutlasses, and upon the table was a decanter of whisky he had unearthed from some mysterious recess, and he was very full of apologies because the soda had run out.

So we sat awhile and quaffed and talked, during which he showed me a favourite rifle, small of bore but of high power and exquisite balance, at sight of which I straightway broke the tenth commandment. He also showed me a portrait of his wife (which I likewise admired), a picture taken by himself and by him developed in some dark nook aboard.

After this, our whisky being duly despatched, we crawled into the air again, to find we were approaching a certain jetty. And now, in the delicate manœuvre of bringing to and making fast, my companions, myself and all else were utterly forgotten, as with voice and hand he issued order on order until, gently as a nesting bird, the destroyer came to her berth and was made fast. Hereupon, having shaken hands all round, he handed us over to other naval men as cheery as he, who in due season brought us to the depôt ship, where luncheon awaited us.

I have dined in many places and have eaten with many different folk, but never have I enjoyed a meal more than this, perhaps because of the padre who presided at my end of the table. A manly cleric this, bright-eyed, resolute of jaw but humorous of mouth, whose white choker did but seem to offset the virility of him. A man, I judged, who preached little and did much—a sailor's padre in very truth.

He told me how, but for an accident, he would have sailed with Admiral Cradock on his last, ill-fated cruise, where so many died that Right and Justice might endure.

"Poor chaps!" said I.

"Yes," said he, gently, "and yet it is surely a noble thing to—die greatly!"

And surely, surely for all those who in cause so just have met Death unflinching and unafraid, who have taken hold upon that which we call Life and carried it through and beyond the portals of Death into a sphere of nobler and greater living—surely to such as these strong souls the Empire they served so nobly and loved so truly will one day enshrine them, their memory and deeds, on the brightest, most glorious page of her history, which shall be a monument more enduring than brass or stone, a monument that shall never pass away.

So we talked of ships and the sea and of men until, aware that the company had risen, we rose also, and donning hats and coats, set forth, talking still. Together we paced beside docks and along piers that stretched away by the mile, massive structures of granite and concrete, which had only come into being, so he told me, since the war.

Side by side we ascended the broad gangway, and side by side we set foot upon that battle-scarred deck whose timbers, here and there, showed the whiter patches of newer wood. Here he turned to give me his hand, after first writing down name and address, and, with mutual wishes of meeting again, went to his duties and left me to the wonders of this great ship.

Crossing the broad deck, more spacious it seemed than an ocean liner, I came where my travelling companions were grouped about a grim memorial of the Jutland battle, a huge projectile that had struck one of the after turrets, in the doing of which it had transformed itself into a great, convoluted disc, and was now mounted as a memento of that tremendous day.

And here it was I became acquainted with my Midshipmite, who looked like an angel of sixteen, bore himself like a veteran, and spoke (when his shyness had worn off a little) like a British fighting man.

To him I preferred the request that he would pilot me over this great vessel, which he (blushing a little) very readily agreed to do. Thereafter, in his wake, I ascended stairways, climbed ladders, wriggled through narrow spaces, writhed round awkward corners, up and ever up.

"It's rather awkward, I'm afraid, sir," said he in his gentle voice, hanging from an iron ladder with one hand and a foot, the better to address me. "You see, we never bring visitors this way as a rule—"

"Good!" said I, crushing my hat on firmer. "The unbeaten track for me—lead on!"

Onward and upward he led until all at once we reached a narrow platform, railed round and hung about with plaited rope screens which he called splinter-mats, over which I had a view of land and water, of ships and basins, of miles of causeways and piers, none of which had been in existence before the war. And immediately below me, far, far down, was the broad white sweep of deck, with the forward turrets where were housed the great guns whose grim muzzles stared patiently upwards, nuzzling the air almost as though scenting another battle.

And standing in this coign of vantage, in my mind's eye I saw this mighty vessel as she had been, the heave of the fathomless sea below, the whirling battle-smoke about her, the air full of the crashing thunder of her guns as she quivered 'neath their discharge. I heard the humming drone of shells coming from afar, a hum that grew to a wail—a shriek—and the sickening crash as they smote her or threw up great waterspouts high as her lofty fighting-tops; I seemed to hear through it all the ring of electric bells from the various fire-controls, and voices calm and all unshaken by the hellish din uttering commands down the many speaking-tubes.

"And you," said I, turning to the youthful figure beside me, "you were in the battle?"

He blushingly admitted that he was.

"And how did you feel?"

He wrinkled his smooth brow and laughed a little shyly.

"Really I—I hardly know, sir."

I asked him if at such times one was not inclined to feel a trifle shaken, a little nervous, or, might one say, afraid?

"Yes, sir," he agreed politely, "I suppose so—only, you see, we were all too jolly busy to think about it!"

"Oh!" said I, taking out a cigarette, "too busy! Of course! I see! And where is the Captain during action, as a rule?"

"As a matter of fact he stood—just where you are, sir. Stood there the whole six hours it was hottest."

"Here!" I exclaimed. "But it is quite exposed."

My Midshipmite, being a hardy veteran in world-shaking naval battles, permitted himself to smile.

"But, you see, sir," he gently explained, "it's really far safer out here than being shut up in a gun-turret or—or down below, on account of er—er—you understand, sir?"

"Oh, quite!" said I, and thereafter thought awhile, and, receiving his ready permission, lighted my cigarette. "I think," said I, as we prepared to descend from our lofty perch, "I'm sure it's just—er— that kind of thing that brought one Francis Drake out of so very many tight corners. By the way—do you smoke?"

My Midshipmite blushingly confessed he did, and helped himself from my case with self-conscious fingers.

Reaching the main deck in due season, I found I had contrived to miss the Chief Gunner's lecture on the great guns, whereupon who so agitated and bitterly apologetic as my Midshipmite, who there and then ushered me hastily down more awkward stairs and through narrow openings into a place of glistening, gleaming polish and furbishment where, beside the shining breech of a monster gun, muscular arm negligently leaning thereon, stood a round-headed, broad-shouldered man, he the presiding genius of this (as I afterwards found) most sacred place.

His lecture was ended and he was addressing a few well-chosen closing remarks in slightly bored fashion (he had showed off his ponderous playthings to divers kings, potentates and bigwigs at home and abroad, I learned) when I, though properly awed by the gun but more especially by the gunner, ventured to suggest that a gun that had been through three engagements and had been fired so frequently must necessarily show some signs of wear. The gunner glanced at me, and I shall never forget that look. With his eyes on mine, he touched a lever in negligent fashion, whereon silently the great breech slipped away with a hiss and whistle of air, and with his gaze always fixed he suggested I might glance down the bore.

Obediently I stooped, whereon he spake on this wise:

"If you cast your heyes to the right abaft the breech you'll observe slight darkening of riflin's. Now glancin' t'left of piece you'll perceive slight darkening of riflin's. Now casting your heyes right forrard you'll re-mark slight roughening of riflin's towards muzzle of piece and—there y'are, sir. One hundred and twenty-seven times she's been fired by my 'and and good for as many more—both of us. Arternoon, gentlemen, and—thank ye!"

Saying which he touched a lever in the same negligent fashion, the mighty breech block slid back into place, and I walked forth humbly into the outer air.

Here I took leave of my Midshipmite, who stood among a crowd of his fellows to watch me down the gangplank, and I followed whither I was led very full of thought, as well I might be, until rousing, I found myself on the deck of that famous *Warspite*, which our foes are so comfortably certain lies a shattered wreck off Jutland. Here I presently fell into discourse with a tall lieutenant, with whom I went alow and aloft; he showed me cockpit, infirmary and engine-room; he showed me the wonder of her steering apparatus, and pointed to the small hand-wheel in the bowels of this huge ship whereby she had been steered limping into port. He directed my gaze also to divers vast shell holes and rents in her steel sides, now very neatly mended by steel plates held in place by many large bolts. Wherever we went were sailors, by the hundred it seemed, and yet I was struck by the size and airy spaciousness between decks.

"The strange thing about the Hun," said my companion, as we mounted upward again, "is that he is so amazingly accurate with his big guns. Anyway, as we steamed into range he registered direct hits time after time, and his misses were so close the spray was flying all over us. Yes, Fritz is wonderfully accurate, but"—here my companion paused to flick some dust from his braided cuff—"but when we began to knock him about a bit it was funny how it rattled him—quite funny, you know. His shots got wider and wider, until they were falling pretty well a mile wide—very funny!" and the lieutenant smiled dreamily. "Fritz will shoot magnificently if you only won't shoot back. But really I don't blame him for thinking he'd sunk us; you see, there were six of 'em potting away at us at one time—couldn't see us for spray—"

"And how did you feel just then?" I enquired.

"Oh, rotten! You see I'd jammed my finger in some tackle for one thing, and just then the light failed us. We'd have bagged the lot if the light had held a little longer. But next time—who knows? Care for a cup of tea?"

"Thanks!" I answered. "But where are the others?"

"Oh, by Jove! I fancy your party's gone—I'll see!"

This proving indeed the case, I perforce took my leave, and with a midshipman to guide me, presently stepped aboard a boat which bore us back beneath the shadow of that mighty bridge stark against the evening sky.

Riding citywards through the deepening twilight I bethought me of the Midshipmite who, amid the roar and tumult of grim battle, had been "too busy" to be afraid; of the round-headed gunner who, like his gun, was ready and eager for more, and of the tall lieutenant who, with death in many awful shapes shrieking and crashing about him, felt "rotten" by reason of a bruised finger and failing light.

And hereupon I felt proud that I, too, was a Briton, of the same breed as these mighty ships and the splendid fellows who man them — these Keepers of the Seas, who in battle as in tempest do their duty unseen, unheard, because it is their duty.

Therefore, all who are so blest as to live within these isles take comfort and courage from this — that despite raging tempest and desperate battle, we, trusting in the justice of our cause, in these iron men and mighty ships, may rest secure, since truly worthy are these, both ships and men, of the glorious traditions of the world's most glorious navy.

But, as they do their duty by Britain and the Empire, let it be our inestimable privilege as fellow Britons to do our duty as nobly both to the Empire and — to them.

VII

A HOSPITAL

The departure platform of a great station (for such as have eyes to see) is always a sad place, but nowadays it is a place of tragedy.

He was tall and thin—a boyish figure—and his khaki-clad arm was close about her slender form. The hour was early and their corner bleak and deserted, thus few were by to heed his stiff-lipped, agonised smile and the passionate clasp of her hands, or to hear her heartbreaking sobs and his brave words of comfort; and I, shivering in the early morning wind, hasted on, awed by a grief that made the grey world greyer.

Very soon London was behind us, and we were whirling through a countryside wreathed in mist wherein I seemed to see a girl's tear-wet cheeks and a boy's lips that smiled so valiantly for all their pitiful quiver; thus I answered my companion somewhat at random and the waiter's proffer of breakfast was an insult. And, as I stared out at misty trees and hedgerow I began as it were to sense a grimness in the very air—the million-sided tragedy of war; behind me the weeping girl, before me and looming nearer with every mile, the Somme battle-front.

At a table hard by a group of clear-eyed subalterns were chatting and laughing over breakfast, and in their merriment I, too, rejoiced. Yet the grimness was with me still as we rocked and swayed through the wreathing mist.

But trains, even on a foggy morning, have a way of getting there at last, so, in due season, were docks and more docks, with the funnels of ships, and beyond these misty shapes upon a misty sea, the gaunt outlines of destroyers that were to convoy us Francewards. Hereupon my companion, K., a hardened traveller, inured to customs, passports and the like noxious things, led me through a jostling throng, his long legs striding rapidly when they found occasion, past rank upon rank of soldiers returning to duty, very neat and orderly, and looking, I thought, a little grim.

Presently the warps were cast off and very soon we were in the lift and roll of the Channel; the white cliffs slowly faded, the wind freshened, and I, observing that every one had donned life belts, forthwith girded on one of the clumsy contrivances also.

In mid-channel it blew hard and the destroyers seemed to be making heavy weather of it, now lost in spray, now showing a glistening height of freeboard, and, as I watched, remembering why they were there, my cumbrous life belt grew suddenly very comfortable.

Came a growing density on the horizon, a blue streak that slowly and little by little grew into roofs, chimneys, docks and shipping, and France was before us, and it was with almost reverent hands that I laid aside my clumsy cork jacket and was presently on French soil. And yet, except for a few chattering porters, the air rang with good English voices hailing each other in cheery greetings, and khaki was everywhere. But now, as I followed my companion's long legs past these serried, dun-coloured ranks, it seemed to me that they held themselves straighter and looked a little more grim even than they had done in England.

I stood, lost in the busy scene before me, when, hearing K.'s voice, I turned to be introduced to Captain R., tall, bright-eyed, immaculate, and very much master of himself and circumstances it seemed, for, despite crowded customs office, he whisked us through and thence before sundry officials, who glared at me and my passport, signed, stamped, returned it and permitted me to go.

After luncheon we drove to a great base hospital where I was introduced to the Colonel-Surgeon in charge, a quiet man, who took us readily under his able guidance. And indeed a huge place was this, a place for me of awe and wonder, the more so as I learned that the greater part of it had come into being within one short year.

It lies beside the sea, this hospital, where clean winds blow, its neat roadways are bordered by green lawns and flanked by long, low buildings that reach away in far perspective, buildings of corrugated iron, of wood and asbestos, a very city, but one where there is no riot and rush of traffic, truly a city of peace and brooding quietude.

And as I looked upon this silent city, my awe grew, for the Colonel, in his gentle voice, spoke of death and wounds, of shell-shock, nerve-wrack and insanity; but he told also of wonderful cures, of miracles performed on those that should have died, and of reason and sanity won back.

"And you?" I questioned, "have you done many such wonders?"

"Few!" he answered, and sighed. "You see, my duties now are chiefly administrative," and he seemed gently grieved that it should be so.

He brought us into wards, long, airy and many-windowed, places of exquisite neatness and order, where calm-faced sisters were busied, and smart, soft-treading orderlies came and went. Here in white cots lay many bandaged forms, some who, propped on pillows, watched us bright-eyed and nodded in cheery greeting; others who lay so ominously still.

But as I passed between the long rows of cots, I was struck with the look of utter peace and content on so many of the faces and wondered, until, remembering the hell whence they had so lately come, I thought I understood. Thus, bethinking me of how these dire hurts had been come by, I took off my hat, and trod between these beds of silent suffering as softly as I could, for these men had surely come "out of great tribulation."

In another ward I saw numbers of German wounded, most of them bearded; many there were who seemed weakly and undersized, and among them were many grey heads, a very motley company. These, the Colonel informed us, received precisely the same treatment as our own wounded, even to tobacco and cigarettes.

We followed our soft-voiced conductor through many other wards where he showed us strange and wondrous devices in splints; he halted us by hanging beds of weird shape and cots that swung on pulleys; he descanted on wounds to flesh and bone and brain, of lives snatched from the grip of Death by the marvels of up-to-date surgery, and as I listened to his pleasant voice I sensed much of the grim wonders he left untold. We visited X-ray rooms and operating theatre against whose walls were glass cases filled with a multitudinous array of instruments for the saving of life, and here it was I learned that in certain cases, a chisel, properly handled, was a far more delicate tool than the finest saw.

"A wonderful place," said I for the hundredth time as we stepped out upon a trim, green lawn. The Colonel-Surgeon smiled.

"It took some planning," he admitted, "a little while ago it was a sandy wilderness."

"But these lawns?" I demurred.

"Came to me of their own accord," he answered. "At least, the seed did, washed ashore from a wreck, so I had it planted and it has done rather well. Now, what else can I show you? It would take all the afternoon to visit every ward, and they are all much alike—but there is the mad ward if you'd care to see that? This way."

A strange place, this, divided into compartments or cubicles where were many patients in the familiar blue overalls, most of whom rose and stood at attention as we entered. Tall, soldierly figures they seemed, and yet with an indefinable something in their looks—a vagueness of gaze, a loose-lipped, too-ready smile, a vacancy of expression. Some there were who scowled sullenly enough, others who sat crouched apart, solitary souls, who, I learned, felt themselves outcast; others again crouched in corners haunted by the dread of a pursuing vengeance always at hand.

One such the Colonel accosted, asking what was wrong. The man looked up, looked down and muttered unintelligibly, whereupon the Sister spoke.

"He believes that every one thinks him a spy," she explained, and touched the man's bowed head with a hand as gentle as her voice.

"Shell-shock is a strange thing," said the Colonel-Surgeon, "and affects men in many extraordinary ways, but seldom permanently."

"You mean that those poor fellows will recover?" I asked.

"Quite ninety per cent," he answered in his quiet, assured voice.

I was shown over laundries complete in every detail; I walked through clothing stores where, in a single day, six hundred men had been equipped from head to foot; I beheld large machines for the sterilisation of garments foul with the grime of battle and other things.

Truly, here, within the hospital that had grown, mushroom-like, within the wild, was everything for the alleviation of hurts and suffering more awful than our fighting ancestors ever had to endure. Presently I left this place, but now, although a clean, fresh wind blew and the setting sun peeped out, the world somehow seemed a grimmer place than ever.

In the Dark Ages, humanity endured much of sin and shame and suffering, but never such as in this age of Reason and Culture. This same earth has known evils of every kind, has heard the screams of outraged innocence, the groan of tortured flesh, and has reddened beneath the heel of Tyranny; this same sun has seen the smoke and ravishment of cities and been darkened by the hateful mists of war—but never such a war as this of cultured barbarity with all its new devilishness. Shell-shock and insanity, poison gas and slow strangulation, liquid fire and poison shells. Rape, Murder, Robbery, Piracy, Slavery—each and every crime is here—never has humanity endured all these horrors together until now.

But remembering by whose will these evils have been loosed upon the world, remembering the innocent blood, the bitter tears, the agony of soul and heartbreak, I am persuaded that Retribution must follow as sure as to-morrow's dawn. The evil that men do lives after them and lives on for ever.

Should they, who have worked for and planned this misery, escape the ephemeral justice of man, there is yet the inexorable tribunal of the Hereafter, which no transgressor, small or great, humble or mighty, may in any wise escape.

VIII
THE GUNS

A fine, brisk morning; a long, tree-bordered road dappled with fugitive sun-beams, making a glory of puddles that leapt in shimmering spray beneath our flying wheels. A long, straight road that ran on and on unswerving, uphill and down, beneath tall, straight trees that flitted past in never-ending procession, and beyond these a rolling, desolate countryside of blue hills and dusky woods; and in the air from beyond this wide horizon a sound that rose above the wind gusts and the noise of our going, a faint whisper that seemed in the air close about us and yet to be of the vague distances, a whisper of sound, a stammering murmur, now rising, now falling, but never quite lost.

In rain-sodden fields to right and left were many figures bent in diligent labour, men in weatherworn, grey-blue uniforms and knee-boots, while on the roadside were men who lounged, or sat smoking cigarettes, rifle across knees and wicked-looking bayonets agleam, wherefore these many German prisoners toiled with the unremitting diligence aforesaid.

The road surface improving somewhat we went at speed and, as we lurched and swayed, the long, straight road grew less deserted. Here and there transport lorries by ones and twos, then whole convoys drawn up beside the road, often axle deep in mud, or lumbering heavily onwards; and ever as we went that ominous, stammering murmur beyond the horizon grew louder and more distinct.

On we went, through scattered villages alive with khaki-clad figures with morions cocked at every conceivable angle, past leafy lanes bright with the wink of long bayonets; through country towns, whose wide squares and narrow, old-world streets rang with the ordered tramp of feet, the stamp of horses and rumble of gun wheels, where ruddy English faces turned to stare and broad khaki backs swung easily beneath their many accoutrements. And in street and square and by-street, always and ever was that murmurous stammer of sound more ominous and threatening, yet which nobody seemed to heed—not even K., my companion, who puffed his cigarette and "was glad it had stopped raining."

So, picking our way through streets a-throng with British faces, dodging guns and limbers, wagons and carts of all descriptions, we came out upon the open road again. And now, there being no surface at all to speak of, we perforce went slow, and I watched where, just in front, a string of lorries lumbered heavily along, pitching and rolling very much like boats in a choppy sea.

Presently we halted to let a column go by, officers a-horse and a-foot with the long files behind, but all alike splashed and spattered with mud. Men, these, who carried their rifles anyhow, who tramped along, rank upon rank, weary men, who showed among them here and there grim evidence of battle—rain-sodden men with hair that clung to muddy brows beneath the sloping brims of muddy helmets; men who tramped ankle-deep in mud and who sang and whistled blithe as birds. So they splashed wearily through the mud, upborne in their fatigue by that indomitable spirit that has always made the Briton the fighting man he is.

At second speed we toiled along again behind the lorries who were making as bad weather of it as ever, when all at once I caught my breath, hearkening to the far, faint skirling of Highland bagpipes, and, leaning from the car, saw before us a company of Highlanders, their mud-splashed knees a-swing together, their khaki kilts swaying in rhythm, their long bayonets a-twinkle, while down the wind came the regular tramp of their feet and the wild, frenzied wailing of their pipes. Soon we were up with them, bronzed, stalwart figures, grim fighters from muddy spatter-dashes to steel helmets, beneath which eyes turned to stare at us—eyes blue and merry, eyes dark and sombre—as they swung along to the lilting music of the pipes.

At the rear the stretcher-bearers marched, the rolled-up stretchers upon their shoulders; but even so, by various dark stains and marks upon that dingy canvas, I knew that here was a company that had done and endured much. Close by me was a man whose hairy knee was black with dried blood—to him I tentatively proffered my cigarette case.

"Wull ye hae one the noo?" I questioned. For a moment he eyed me a trifle dour and askance, then he smiled (a grave Scots smile).

"Thank ye, I wull that!" said he, and extracted the cigarette with muddy fingers.

"Ye'll hae a sore leg, I'm thinking!" said I.

"Ou aye," he admitted with the same grave smile, "but it's no sae muckle as a' that—juist a wee bit skelpit I—"

Our car moved forward, gathered speed, and we bumped and swayed on our way; the bagpipes shrieked and wailed, grew plaintively soft, and were drowned and lost in that other sound which was a murmur no longer, but a rolling, distant thunder, with occasional moments of silence.

"Ah, the guns at last!" said I.

"Yes," nodded K., lighting another cigarette, "I've been listening to them for the last hour."

Here my friend F., who happened to be the Intelligence Officer in charge, leaned forward to say:

"I'm afraid we can't get into Beaumont Hamel, the Boches are strafing it rather, this morning, but we'll go as near as we can get, and then on to what was La Boiselle. We shall leave the car soon, so better get into your tin hats." Forthwith I buckled on one of the morions we had brought for the purpose and very uncomfortable I found it. Having made it fairly secure, I turned, grinning furtively, to behold K.'s classic features crowned with his outlandish-seeming headgear, and presently caught him grinning furtively at mine.

"They're not so heavy as I expected," said I.

"About half a pound," he suggested.

Pulling up at a shell-shattered village we left the car and trudged along a shell-torn road, along a battered and rusty railway line, and presently struck into a desolate waste intersected by sparse hedgerows and with here and there desolate, leafless trees, many of which, in shattered trunk and broken bough, showed grim traces of what had been; and ever as we advanced these ugly scars grew more frequent, and we were continually dodging sullen pools that were the work of bursting shells. And then it began to rain again.

On we went, splashing through puddles, slipping in mud, and ever as we went my boots and my uncomfortable helmet grew heavier and heavier, while in the heaven above, in the earth below and in the air about us was the quiver and thunder of unseen guns. As we stumbled through the muddy desolation I beheld wretched hovels wherein khaki-clad forms moved, and from one of these damp and dismal structures a merry whistling issued, with hoarse laughter.

On we tramped, through rain and mud, which, like my helmet, seemed to grow momentarily heavier.

"K.," said I, as he floundered into a shell hole, "about how heavy did you say these helmets were?"

"About a pound!" said he, fierce-eyed. "Confound the mud!"

Away to our left and high in air a puff of smoke appeared, a pearl-grey, fleecy cloud, and as I, unsuspecting, watched it writhe into fantastic shapes, my ears were smitten with a deafening report, and instinctively I ducked.

"Shrapnel!" said F., waving his hand in airy introduction. "They're searching the road yonder I expect—ah, there goes another! Yes, they're trying the road yonder—but here's the trench—in with you!"

I am free to confess that I entered that trench precipitately—so hurriedly, in fact, that my helmet fell off, and, as I replaced it, I was not sorry to see that this trench was very deep and narrow. As we progressed, very slowly by reason of clinging mud, F. informed us that this trench had been our old front line before we took Beaumont Hamel; and I noticed many things, as, clips of cartridges, unexploded bombs, Lewis-gun magazines, parts of a broken machine gun, and various odds and ends of accoutrements. In some places this trench had fallen in because of rain and other things and was almost impassable, wherefore, after much floundering and splashing, F. suggested we should climb out again, which we did forthwith, very moist and muddy.

And thus at last I looked at that wide stretch of country across which our men had advanced unshaken and undismayed, through a hell the like of which the world had never known before; and, as I stood there, I could almost see those long, advancing waves of khaki-clad figures, their ranks swept by the fire of countless rifles and machine guns, pounded by high explosives, blasted by withering shrapnel, lost in the swirling death-mist of poison gas—heroic ranks which, rent asunder, shattered, torn, yet swung steadily on through smoke and flame, unflinching and unafraid. As if to make the picture more real, came the thunderous crash of a shell behind us, but this time I forgot to duck.

Far in front of us I saw a huge puff of smoke, and as it thinned out beheld clouds of earth and broken beams that seemed to hang suspended a moment ere they fell and vanished. After a moment came another puff of smoke further to our right, and beyond this another, and again, beyond this, another.

"A battery of heavies," said F.

Even as he spoke the four puffs burst forth again and upon exactly the same ground.

At this juncture a head appeared over the parapet behind us and after some talk with F., came one who tendered us a pair of binoculars, by whose aid I made out the British new line of trenches which had once been German. So I stood, dry-mouthed, to watch the burst of those huge shells exploding upon our British line. Fascinated, I stared until F.'s hand on my arm aroused me, and returning the glasses with a hazy word of thanks I followed my companions, though often turning to watch the shooting which now I thought much too good.

And now we were traversing the great battlefield where, not long since, so many of our bravest had fallen that Britain might still be Britain. Even yet, upon its torn and trampled surface I could read something of the fight—here a broken shoulder belt, there a cartridge pouch, yonder a stained and tattered coat, while everywhere lay bombs, English and German.

"If you want to see La Boiselle properly we must hurry!" said F., and off he went at the double with K.'s long legs striding beside him, but, as for me, I must needs turn for one last look where those deadly smoke puffs came and went with such awful regularity.

The rain had stopped, but it was three damp and mud-spattered wretches who clambered back into the waiting car.

"K.," said I, as we removed our cumbrous headgear, "about how much do you suppose these things weigh?"

"Fully a ton!" he answered, jerking his cap over his eyes and scowlingly accepting a cigarette.

Very soon the shattered village was far behind and we were threading a devious course between huge steam-tractors, guns, motor-lorries and more guns. We passed soldiers a-horse and a-foot and long strings of ambulance cars; to right and left of the road were artillery parks and great camps, that stretched away into the distance. Here also were vast numbers of the ubiquitous motor-lorry with many three-wheeled tractors for the big guns. We sped past hundreds of horses picketed in long lines; past countless tents smeared crazily in various coloured paints; past huts little and huts big; past swamps knee-deep in mud where muddy men were taking down or setting up other tents. On we sped through all the confused order of a mighty army, until, chancing to raise my eyes aloft, I beheld a huge balloon, which, as I watched, mounted up and up into the air.

"One of our sausages!" said F., gloved hand waving. "Plenty of 'em round here; see, there's another in that cloud, and beyond it another."

So for a while I rode with my eyes turned upwards, and thus I presently saw far ahead many aeroplanes that flew in strange, zigzag fashion, now swooping low, now climbing high, now twisting and turning giddily.

"Some of our 'planes under fire!" said F., "you can see the shrapnel bursting all around 'em—there's the smoke—we call 'em woolly bears. Won't see any Boche 'planes, though—rather not!"

Amidst all these wonders and marvels our fleet car sped on, jolting and lurching violently over ruts, pot-holes and the like until we came to a part of the road where many men were engaged with pick and shovel; and here, on either side of the highway, I noticed many grim-looking heaps and mounds—ugly, shapeless dumps, depressing in their very hideousness. Beside one such unlovely dump our car pulled up, and F., gloved finger pointing, announced:

"The Church of La Boiselle. That heap you see yonder was once the Mairie, and beyond, the schoolhouse. The others were houses and cottages. Oh, La Boiselle was quite a pretty place once. We get out here to visit the guns—this way."

Obediently I followed whither he led, nothing speaking, for surely here was matter beyond words. Leaving the road, we floundered over what seemed like ash heaps, but which had once been German trenches faced and reinforced by concrete and steel plates. Many of these last lay here and there, awfully bent and twisted, but of trenches I saw none save a few yards here and there half filled with indescribable débris. It was, indeed, a place of horror—a frightful desolation beyond all words. Everywhere about us were signs of dreadful death—they came to one in the very air, in lowering heaven and tortured earth. Far as the eye could reach the ground was pitted with great shell holes, so close that they broke into one another and formed horrid pools full of shapeless things within the slime.

Across this hellish waste I went cautiously by reason of torn and twisted tangles of German barbed wire, of hand grenades and huge shells, of broken and rusty iron and steel that once were deadly machine guns. As I picked my way among all this flotsam, I turned to take up a bayonet, slipped in the slime and sank to my waist in a shell hole—even then I didn't touch bottom, but scrambled out, all grey mud from waist down—but I had the bayonet.

It was in this woeful state that I shook hands with the Major of the battery. And as we stood upon that awful waste, he chattered, I remember, of books. Then, side by side, we came to the battery—four mighty howitzers, that crashed and roared and shook the very earth with each discharge, and whose shells roared through the air with the rush of a dozen express trains.

Following the Major's directing finger, I fixed my gaze some distance above the muzzle of the nearest gun and, marvel of marvels, beheld that dire messenger of death and destruction rush forth, soaring, upon its way, up and up, until it was lost in cloud. Time after time I saw the huge shells leap skywards and vanish on their long journey, and stood thus lost in wonder, and as I watched I could not but remark on the speed and dexterity with which the crews handled these monstrous engines.

"Yes," nodded the Major, "strange thing is that a year ago they *weren't*, you know—guns weren't in existence and the men weren't gunners—clerks an' all that sort of thing, you know—civilians, what?"

"They're pretty good gunners now—judging by effect!" said I, nodding towards the abomination of desolation that had once been a village.

"Rather!" nodded the Major, cheerily, "used to think it took three long years to make a gunner once—do it in six short months now! Pretty good going for old England, what? How about a cup of tea in my dugout?"

But evening was approaching, and having far to go we had perforce to refuse his hospitality and bid him a reluctant good-by.

"Don't forget to take a peep at the mine craters," said he, and waving a cheery adieu, vanished into his dugout.

Ten minutes' walk, along the road, and before us rose a jagged mount, and beyond it another, uncanny hills, seared and cracked and sinister, up whose steep slopes I scrambled and into whose yawning depths I gazed in awestruck wonder; so deep, so wide and huge of circumference, it seemed rather the result of some titanic convulsion of nature than the handiwork of man.

I could imagine the cataclysmic roar of the explosion, the smoke and flame of the mighty upheaval and war found for me yet another horror as I turned and descended the precipitous slope. Now, as I went, I stumbled over a small mound, then halted all at once, for at one end of this was a very small cross, rudely constructed and painted white, and tacked to this a strip of lettered tin, bearing a name and number, and beneath these the words, "One of the best." So I took off my hat and stood awhile beside that lonely mound of muddy earth ere I went my way.

Slowly our car lurched onward through the waste, and presently on either side the way I saw other such mounds and crosses, by twos and threes, by fifties, by hundreds, in long rows beyond count. And looking around me on this dreary desolation I knew that one day (since nothing dies) upon this place of horror grass would grow and flowers bloom again; along this now desolate and deserted road people would come by the thousand; these humble crosses and mounds of muddy earth would become to all Britons a holy place where so many of our best and bravest lie, who, undismayed, have passed through the portals of Death into the fuller, greater, nobler living.

Full of such thoughts I turned for one last look, and then I saw that the setting sun had turned each one of these humble little crosses into things of shining glory.

IX
A TRAINING CAMP

The great training camp lay, a rain-lashed wilderness of windy levels and bleak, sandy hills, range upon range, far as the eye could see, with never a living thing to break the monotony. But presently, as our car lurched and splashed upon its way, there rose a sound that grew and grew, the awesome sound of countless marching feet.

On they came, these marching men, until we could see them by the hundred, by the thousand, their serried ranks stretching away and away until they were lost in distance. Scots were here, Lowland and Highland; English and Irish were here, with bronzed New Zealanders, adventurous Canadians and hardy Australians; men, these, who had come joyfully across half the world to fight, and, if need be, die for those ideals which have made the Empire assuredly the greatest and mightiest this world has ever known. And as I listened to the rhythmic tramp of these countless feet, it seemed like the voice of this vast Empire proclaiming to the world that Wrong and Injustice must cease among the nations; that man, after all, despite all the "Frightfulness" that warped intelligence may conceive, is yet faithful to the highest in him, faithful to that deathless, purposeful determination that Right shall endure, the abiding belief of which has brought him through the dark ages, through blood and misery and shame, on his progress ever upward.

So, while these men of the Empire tramped past through blinding rain and wind, our car stopped before a row of low-lying wooden buildings, whence presently issued a tall man in rain-sodden trench cap and burberry, who looked at me with a pair of very dark, bright eyes and gripped my hand in hearty clasp.

He was apologetic because of the rain, since, as he informed us, he had just ordered all men to their quarters, and thus I should see nothing doing in the training line; nevertheless he cheerfully offered to show us over the camp, despite mud and wind and rain, and to explain things as fully as he could; whereupon we as cheerfully accepted.

The wind whistled about us, the rain pelted us, but the Major heeded it nothing—neither did I—while K. loudly congratulated himself on having come in waders and waterproof hat, as, through mud and mire, through puddles and clogging sand, we followed the Major's long boots, crossing bare plateaux, climbing precipitous slopes, leaping trenches, slipping and stumbling, while ever the Major talked, wherefore I heeded not wind or rain, for the Major talked well.

He descanted on the new and horribly vicious methods of bayonet fighting—the quick thrust and lightning recovery; struggling with me upon a sandy, rain-swept height, he showed me how, in wrestling for your opponent's rifle, the bayonet is the thing. He halted us before devilish contrivances of barbed wire, each different from the other, but each just as ugly. He made us peep through loopholes, each and every different from the other, yet each and every skilfully hidden from an enemy's observation. We stood beside trenches of every shape and kind while he pointed out their good and bad points; he brought us to a place where dummy figures had been set up, their rags a-flutter, forlorn objects in the rain.

"Here," said he, "is where we teach 'em to throw live bombs—you can see where they've been exploding; dummies look a bit off-colour, don't they?" And he pointed to the ragged scarecrows with his whip. "You know, I suppose," he continued, "that a Mills' bomb is quite safe until you take out the pin, and then it is quite safe as long as you hold it, but the moment it is loosed the lever flies off, which releases the firing lever and in a few seconds it explodes. It is surprising how men vary; some are born bombers, some soon learn, but some couldn't be bombers if they tried—not that they're cowards, it's just a case of mentality. I've seen men take hold of a bomb, pull out the pin, and then stand with the thing clutched in their fingers, absolutely unable to move! And there they'd stand till Lord knows when if the Sergeant didn't take it from them. I remember a queer case once. We were saving the pins to rig up dummy bombs, and the order was: 'Take the bomb in your right hand, remove the pin, put the pin in your pocket, and at the word of command, throw the bomb.' Well, this particular fellow was so wrought up that he threw away the pin and put the bomb in his pocket!"

"Was he killed?" I asked.

"No. The sergeant just had time to dig the thing out of the man's pocket and throw it away. Bomb exploded in the air and knocked 'em both flat."

"Did the sergeant get the V.C. or M.C. or anything?" I enquired.

The Major smiled and shook his head.

"I have a good many sergeants here and they can't all have 'em! Now come and see my lecture theatres."

Presently, looming through the rain, I saw huge circular structures that I could make nothing of, until, entering the larger of the two, I stopped in surprise, for I looked down into a huge, circular amphitheatre, with circular rows of seats descending tier below tier to a circular floor of sand, very firm and hard.

"All made out of empty oil cans!" said the Major, tapping the nearest can with his whip. "I have 'em filled with sand and stacked as you see!—good many thousands of 'em here. Find it good for sound too—shout and try! This place holds about five thousand men—"

"Whose wonderful idea was this?"

"Oh, just a little wheeze of my own. Now, how about the poison gas; feel like going through it?"

I glanced at K., K. glanced at me. I nodded, so did K.

"Certainly!" said I. Wherefore the Major led us over sandy hills and along sandy valleys and so to a dingy and weatherworn hut, in whose dingy interior we found a bright-faced subaltern in dingy uniform and surrounded by many dingy boxes and a heterogeneous collection of things. The subaltern was busy at work on a bomb with a penknife, while at his elbow stood a sergeant grasping a screwdriver, who, perceiving the Major, came to attention, while the cheery sub. rose, beaming.

"Can you give us some gas?" enquired the Major, after we had been introduced, and had shaken hands.

"Certainly, sir!" nodded the cheerful sub. "Delighted!"

"You might explain something about it, if you will," suggested the Major. "Bombs and gas is your line, you know."

The sub. beamed, and giving certain directions to his sergeant, spake something on this wise.

"Well, 'Frightful Fritz'—I mean the Boches, y'know, started bein' frightful some time ago, y'know—playin' their little tricks with gas an' tear-shells an' liquid fire an' that, and we left 'em to it. Y'see, it wasn't cricket—wasn't playin' the game—what! But Fritz kept at it and was happy as a bird, till one day we woke up an' started bein' frightful too, only when we did begin we were frightfuller than ever Fritz thought of bein'—yes, rather! Our gas is more deadly, our lachrymatory shells are more lachrymose an' our liquid fire's quite tophole—won't go out till it burns out—rather not! So Frightful Fritz is licked at his own dirty game. I've tried his and I've tried ours, an' I know."

Here the sergeant murmured deferentially into the sub.'s ear, whereupon he beamed again and nodded.

"Everything's quite ready!" he announced, "so if you're on?"

Here, after a momentary hesitation, I signified I was, whereupon our sub. grew immensely busy testing sundry ugly, grey flannel gas helmets, fitted with staring eye-pieces of talc and with a hideous snout in front.

Having duly fitted on these clumsy things and buttoned them well under our coat collars, having shown us how we must breathe out through the mouthpiece which acts as a kind of exhaust, our sub. donned his own headpiece, through which his cheery voice reached me in muffled tones:

"You'll feel a kind of ticklin' feelin' in the throat at first, but that's all O.K.—only the chemical the flannel's saturated with. Now follow me, please, an' would you mind runnin', the rain's apt to weaken the solution. This way!"

Dutifully we hasted after him, ploughing through the wet sand, until we came to a heavily timbered doorway that seemingly opened into the hillside, and, beyond this yawning doorway I saw a thick, greenish-yellow mist, a fog exactly the colour of strong absinthe; and then we were in it. K.'s tall figure grew blurred, indistinct, faded utterly away, and I was alone amid that awful, swirling vapour that held death in such agonising form.

I will confess I was not happy, my throat was tickling provokingly, I began to cough and my windpipe felt too small. I hastened forward, but, even as I went, the light grew dimmer and the swirling fog more dense. I groped blindly, began to run, stumbled, and in that moment my hand came in contact with an unseen rope. On I went into gloom, into blackness, until I was presently aware of my companions in front and mightily glad of it. In a while, still following this invisible rope, we turned a corner, the fog grew less opaque, thinned away to a green mist, and we were out in the daylight again, and thankful was I to whip off my stifling helmet and feel the clean wind in my hair and the beat of rain upon my face.

"Notice the ticklin' feelin'?" enquired our sub., as he took our helmets and put them carefully by. "Bit tryin' at first, but you soon get used to it—yes, rather. Some of the men funk tryin' at first—and some hold their breath until they fairly well burst, an' some won't go in at all, so we carry 'em in. That gas you've tried is about twenty times stronger than we get it in the open, but these helmets are a rippin' dodge till the chemical evaporates, then, of course, they're no earthly. This is the latest device—quite a tophole scheme!" And he showed us a box-like contrivance which, when in use, is slung round the neck.

"Are you often in the gas?" I enquired.

"Every day—yes, rather!"

"For how long?"

"Well, I stayed in once for five hours on end—"

"Five hours!" I exclaimed, aghast.

"Y'see, I was experimentin'!"

"And didn't you feel any bad effects?"

"Yes, rather! I was simply dyin' for a smoke. Like to try a lachrymatory?" he enquired, reaching up to a certain dingy box.

"Yes," said I, glancing at K. "Oh, yes, if—"

"Only smart for the time bein'," our sub. assured me. "Make you weep a bit!" Here from the dingy box he fished a particularly vicious-looking bomb and fell to poking at it with a screwdriver. I immediately stepped back. So did K. The Major pulled his moustache and flicked a chunk of mud from his boot with his whip.

"Er—I suppose that thing's all right?" he enquired.

"Oh, yes, quite all right, sir, quite all right," nodded the sub., using the screwdriver as a hammer. "Only wants a little fixin'."

As I watched that deadly thing, for the second time I felt distinctly unhappy; however, the refractory pin, or whatever it was, being fixed to his satisfaction, our sub. led the way out of the dingy hut and going some few paces ahead, paused.

"I'm goin' to give you a liquid-fire bomb first!" said he. "Watch!"

He drew back his hand and hurled the bomb. Almost immediately there was a shattering report and the air was full of thick, grey smoke and yellow flame, smoke that rolled heavily along the ground towards us, flame that burned ever fiercer, fiery yellow tongues that leapt from the sand here and there, that writhed in the wind-gusts, but never diminished.

"Stoop down!" cried the sub., suiting the action to word, "stoop down and get a mouthful of that smoke—makes you jolly sick and unconscious in no time if you get enough of it. Tophole bomb, that— what!"

Then he brought us where those yellow flames leapt and hissed; some of these he covered with wet sand, and lo! they had ceased to be; but the moment the sand was kicked away up they leapt again fiercer than ever.

"We use 'em for bombing Boche dugouts now!" said he; and remembering the dugouts I had seen, I could picture the awful fate of those within, the choking fumes, the fire-scorched bodies! Truly the exponents of Frightfulness have felt the recoil of their own vile methods.

"This is a lachrymatory!" said the sub., whisking another bomb from his pocket. "When it pops, run forward and get in the smoke. It'll sting a bit, but don't rub the tears away—let 'em flow. Don't touch your eyes, it'll only inflame 'em—just weep! Ready? One, two, three!" A second explosion louder than the first, a puff of blue smoke into which I presently ran and then uttered a cry. So sharp, so excruciating was the pain, that instinctively I raised hand to eyes but checked myself, and with tears gushing over my cheeks, blind and agonised, I stumbled away from that hellish vapour. Very soon the pain diminished, was gone, and looking up through streaming tears I beheld the sub. nodding and beaming approval.

"Useful things, eh?" he remarked. "A man can't shed tears and shoot straight, an' he can't weep and fight well, both at the same time— what? Fritz can be very frightful, but we can be more so when we want—yes, rather. The Boches have learned that there's no monopoly in Frightfulness."

In due season we shook hands with our cheery sub., and left him beaming after us from the threshold of the dingy hut.

Britain has been called slow, old-fashioned, and behind the times, but to-day she is awake and at work to such mighty purpose that her once small army is now numbered by the million, an army second to none in equipment or hardy and dauntless manhood.

From her Home Counties, from her Empire beyond the Seas, her millions have arisen, brothers in arms henceforth, bonded together by a spirit of noble self-sacrifice—men grimly determined to suffer wounds and hardship and death itself, that for those who come after them, the world may be a better place and humanity may never again be called upon to endure all the agony and heartbreak of this generation.

X
ARRAS

It was raining, and a chilly wind blew as we passed beneath a battered arch into the tragic desolation of Arras.

I have seen villages pounded by gun-fire into hideous mounds of dust and rubble, their very semblance blasted utterly away; but Arras, shell-torn, scarred, disfigured for all time, is a city still—a City of Desolation. Her streets lie empty and silent, her once pleasant squares are a dreary desolation, her noble buildings, monuments of her ancient splendour, are ruined beyond repair. Arras is a dead city, whose mournful silence is broken only by the intermittent thunder of the guns.

Thus, as I paced these deserted streets where none moved save myself (for my companions had hastened on), as I gazed on ruined buildings that echoed mournfully to my tread, what wonder that my thoughts were gloomy as the day itself? I paused in a street of fair, tall houses, from whose broken windows curtains of lace, of plush, and tapestry flapped mournfully in the chill November wind like rags upon a corpse, while from some dim interior came the hollow rattle of a door, and, in every gust, a swinging shutter groaned despairingly on rusty hinge.

And as I stood in this narrow street, littered with the brick and masonry of desolate homes, and listened to these mournful sounds, I wondered vaguely what had become of all those for whom this door had been wont to open, where now were the eyes that had looked down from these windows many and many a time—would they ever behold again this quiet, narrow street, would these scarred walls echo again to those same voices and ring with joy of life and familiar laughter?

And now this desolate city became as it were peopled with the souls of these exiles; they flitted ghostlike in the dimness behind flapping curtains, they peered down through closed jalousies—wraiths of the men and women and children who had lived and loved and played here before the curse of the barbarian had driven them away.

And, as if to help this illusion, I saw many things that were eloquent of these vanished people—glimpses through shattered windows and beyond demolished house-fronts; here a table set for dinner, with plates and tarnished cutlery on a dingy cloth that stirred damp and lazily in the wind, yonder a grand piano, open and with sodden music drooping from its rest; here again chairs drawn cosily together.

Wherever I looked were evidences of arrested life, of action suddenly stayed; in one bedroom a trunk open, with a pile of articles beside it in the act of being packed; in another, a great bed, its sheets and blankets tossed askew by hands wild with haste; while in a room lined with bookcases a deep armchair was drawn up to the hearth, with a small table whereon stood a decanter and a half-emptied glass, and an open book whose damp leaves stirred in the wind, now and then, as if touched by phantom fingers. Indeed, more than once I marvelled to see how, amid the awful wreckage of broken floors and tumbled ceilings, delicate vases and chinaware had miraculously escaped destruction. Upon one cracked wall a large mirror reflected the ruin of a massive carved sideboard, while in another house, hard by, a magnificent ivory and ebony crucifix yet hung above an awful twisted thing that had been a brass bedstead.

Here and there, on either side this narrow street, ugly gaps showed where houses had once stood, comfortable homes, now only unsightly heaps of rubbish, a confusion of broken beams and rafters, amid which divers familiar objects obtruded themselves, broken chairs and tables, a grandfather clock, and a shattered piano whose melody was silenced for ever.

Through all these gloomy relics of a vanished people I went slow-footed and heedless of direction, until by chance I came out into the wide Place and saw before me all that remained of the stately building which for centuries had been the Hotel de Ville, now nothing but a crumbling ruin of noble arch and massive tower; even so, in shattered façade and mullioned window one might yet see something of that beauty which had made it famous.

Oblivious of driving rain I stood bethinking me of this ancient city: how in the dark ages it had endured the horrors of battle and siege, had fronted the catapults of Rome, heard the fierce shouts of barbarian assailants, known the merciless savagery of religious wars, and remained a city still only for the cultured barbarian of to-day to make of it a desolation.

Very full of thought I turned away, but, as I crossed the desolate square, I was aroused by a voice that hailed me, seemingly from beneath my feet, a voice that echoed eerily in that silent Place. Glancing about I beheld a beshawled head that rose above the littered pavement, and, as I stared, the head nodded and smiling wanly, accosted me again.

Coming thither I looked into a square opening with a flight of steps leading down into a subterranean chamber, and upon these steps a woman sat knitting busily. She enquired if I wished to view the catacombs, and pointed where a lamp burned above another opening and other steps descended lower yet, seemingly into the very bowels of the earth. To her I explained that my time was limited and all I wished to see lay above ground, and from her I learned that some few people yet remained in ruined Arras, who, even as she, lived underground, since every day at irregular intervals the enemy fired into the town haphazard. Only that very morning, she told me, another shell had struck the poor Hotel de Ville, and she pointed to a new, white scar upon the shapeless tower. She also showed me an ugly rent upon a certain wall near by, made by the shell which had killed her husband. Yes, she lived all alone now, she told me, waiting for that good day when the Boches should be driven beyond the Rhine, waiting until the townsfolk should come back and Arras wake to life again: meantime she knitted.

Presently I saluted this solitary woman, and, turning away, left her amid the desolate ruin of that once busy square, her beshawled head bowed above feverishly busy fingers, left her as I had found her— waiting.

And now as I traversed those deserted streets it seemed that this seemingly dead city did but swoon after all, despite its many grievous wounds, for here was life even as the woman had said; evidences of which I saw here and there, in battered stovepipes that had writhed themselves snake-like through rusty cellar gratings and holes in wall or pavement, miserable contrivances at best, whose fumes blackened the walls whereto they clung. Still, nowhere was there sound or sight of folk save in one small back street, where, in a shop that apparently sold everything, from pickles to picture postcards, two British soldiers were buying a pair of braces from a smiling, haggard-eyed woman, and being extremely polite about it in cryptic Anglo-French; and here I foregathered with my companions. Our way led us through the railway station, a much-battered ruin, its clock tower half gone, its platforms cracked and splintered, the iron girders of its great, domed roof bent and twisted, and with never a sheet of glass anywhere. Between the rusty tracks grass and weeds grew and flourished, and the few waybills and excursion placards which still showed here and there looked unutterably forlorn. In the booking office was a confusion of broken desks, stools and overthrown chairs, the floor littered with sodden books and ledgers, but the racks still held thousands of tickets, bearing so many names they might have taken any one anywhere throughout fair France once, but now, it seemed, would never take any one anywhere.

All at once, through the battered swing doors, marched a company of soldiers, the tramp of their feet and the lilt of their voices filling the place with strange echoes, for, being wet and weary and British, they sang cheerily. Packs a-swing, rifles on shoulder, they tramped through shell-torn waiting room and booking hall and out again into wind and wet, and I remember the burden of their chanting was: "Smile! Smile! Smile!"

In a little while I stood amid the ruins of the great cathedral; its mighty pillars, chipped and scarred, yet rose high in air, but its long aisles were choked with rubble and fallen masonry, while through the gaping rents of its lofty roof the rain fell, wetting the shattered heap of particoloured marble that had been the high altar once. Here and there, half buried in the débris at my feet, I saw fragments of memorial tablets, a battered corona, the twisted remains of a great candelabrum, and over and through this mournful ruin a cold and rising wind moaned fitfully. Silently we clambered back over the mountain of débris and hurried on, heedless of the devastation around, heartsick with the gross barbarity of it all.

They tell me that churches and cathedrals must of necessity be destroyed since they generally serve as observation posts. But I have seen many ruined churches—usually beautified by Time and hallowed by tradition—that by reason of site and position could never have been so misused—and then there is the beautiful Chateau d'Eau!

Evening was falling, and as the shadows stole upon this silent city, a gloom unrelieved by any homely twinkle of light, these dreadful streets, these stricken homes took on an aspect more sinister and forbidding in the half-light. Behind those flapping curtains were pits of gloom full of unimagined terrors whence came unearthly sounds, stealthy rustlings, groans and sighs and sobbing voices. If ghosts did flit behind those crumbling walls, surely they were very sad and woeful ghosts.

"Damn this rain!" murmured K. gently.

"And the wind!" said F., pulling up his collar. "Listen to it! It's going to play the very deuce with these broken roofs and things if it blows hard. Going to be a beastly night, and a forty-mile drive in front of us. Listen to that wind! Come on—let's get away!"

Very soon, buried in warm rugs, we sped across dim squares, past wind-swept ruins, under battered arch, and the dismal city was behind us, but, for a while, her ghosts seemed all about us still.

As we plunged on through the gathering dark, past rows of trees that leapt at us and were gone, it seemed to me that the soul of Arras was typified in that patient, solitary woman who sat amid desolate ruin—waiting for the great Day; and surely her patience cannot go unrewarded. For since science has proved that nothing can be utterly destroyed, since I for one am convinced that the soul of man through death is but translated into a fuller and more infinite living, so do I think that one day the woes of Arras shall be done away, and she shall rise again, a City greater perhaps and fairer than she was.

XI

THE BATTLEFIELDS

To all who sit immune, far removed from war and all its horrors, to those to whom when Death comes, he comes in shape as gentle as he may—to all such I dedicate these tales of the front.

How many stories of battlefields have been written of late, written to be scanned hastily over the breakfast table or comfortably lounged over in an easy-chair, stories warranted not to shock or disgust, wherein the reader may learn of the glorious achievements of our armies, of heroic deeds and noble self-sacrifice, so that frequently I have heard it said that war, since it produces heroes, is a goodly thing, a necessary thing.

Can the average reader know or even faintly imagine the other side of the picture? Surely not, for no clean human mind can compass all the horror, all the brutal, grotesque obscenity of a modern battlefield. Therefore I propose to write plainly, briefly, of that which I saw on my last visit to the British front; for since in blood-sodden France men are dying even as I pen these lines, it seems only just that those of us for whom they are giving their lives should at least know something of the manner of their dying. To this end I visited four great battlefields and I would that all such as cry up war, its necessity, its inevitability, might have gone beside me. Though I have sometimes written of war, yet I am one that hates war, one to whom the sight of suffering and bloodshed causes physical pain, yet I forced myself to tread those awful fields of death and agony, to look upon the ghastly aftermath of modern battle, that, if it be possible, I might by my testimony in some small way help those who know as little of war as I did once, to realise the horror of it, that loathing it for the hellish thing it is, they may, one and all, set their faces against war henceforth, with an unshakeable determination that never again shall it be permitted to maim, to destroy and blast out of being the noblest works of God.

What I write here I set down deliberately, with no idea of phrase-making, of literary values or rounded periods; this is and shall be a plain, trite statement of fact.

And now, one and all, come with me in spirit, lend me your mind's eyes, and see for yourselves something of what modern war really is.

Behold then a stretch of country—a sea of mud far as the eye can reach, a grim desolate expanse, its surface ploughed and churned by thousands of high-explosive shells into ugly holes and tortured heaps like muddy waves struck motionless upon this muddy sea. The guns are silent, the cheers and frenzied shouts, the screams and groans have long died away, and no sound is heard save the noise of my own going.

The sun shone palely and a fitful wind swept across the waste, a noxious wind, cold and dank, that chilled me with a sudden dread even while the sweat ran from me. I walked amid shell craters, sometimes knee-deep in mud; I stumbled over rifles half buried in the slime, on muddy knapsacks, over muddy bags half full of rusty bombs, and so upon the body of a dead German soldier. With arms wide-flung and writhen legs grotesquely twisted he lay there beneath my boot, his head half buried in the mud, even so I could see that the maggots had been busy, though the ....[1] had killed them where they clung. So there he lay, this dead Boche, skull gleaming under shrunken scalp, an awful, eyeless thing, that seemed to start, to stir and shiver as the cold wind stirred his muddy clothing. Then nausea and a deadly faintness seized me, but I shook it off, and shivering, sweating, forced myself to stoop and touch that awful thing, and, with the touch, horror and faintness passed, and in their place I felt a deep and passionate pity, for all he was a Boche, and with pity in my heart I turned and went my way.

But now, wherever I looked were other shapes, that lay in attitudes frightfully contorted, grotesque and awful. Here the battle had raged desperately. I stood in a very charnel-house of dead. From a mound of earth upflung by a bursting shell a clenched fist, weather-bleached and pallid, seemed to threaten me; from another emerged a pair of crossed legs with knees up-drawn, very like the legs of one who dozes gently on a hot day. Hard by, a pair of German knee-boots topped a shell crater, and drawing near, I saw the grey-green breeches, belt and pouches, and beyond—nothing but unspeakable corruption. I started back in horror and stepped on something that yielded underfoot—glanced down and saw a bloated, discoloured face, that, even as I looked, vanished beneath my boot and left a bare and grinning skull.

Once again the faintness seized me, and lifting my head I stared round about me and across the desolation of this hellish waste. Far in the distance was the road where men moved to and fro, busy with picks and shovels, and some sang and some whistled and never sound more welcome. Here and there across these innumerable shell holes, solitary figures moved, men, these, who walked heedfully and with heads down-bent. And presently I moved on, but now, like these distant figures, I kept my gaze upon that awful mud lest again I should trample heedlessly on something that had once lived and loved and laughed. And they lay everywhere, here stark and stiff, with no pitiful earth to hide their awful corruption—here again, half buried in slimy mud; more than once my nailed boot uncovered mouldering tunic or things more awful. And as I trod this grisly place my pity grew, and with pity a profound wonder that the world with its so many millions of reasoning minds should permit such things to be, until I remembered that few, even the most imaginative, could realise the true frightfulness of modern men-butchering machinery, and my wonder changed to a passionate desire that such things should be recorded and known, if only in some small measure, wherefore it is I write these things.

I wandered on past shell holes, some deep in slime, that held nameless ghastly messes, some a-brim with bloody water, until I came where three men lay side by side, their hands upon their levelled rifles. For a moment I had the foolish thought that these men were weary and slept, until, coming near, I saw that these had died by the same shell-burst. Near them lay yet another shape, a mangled heap, one muddy hand yet grasping muddy rifle, while, beneath the other lay the fragment of a sodden letter—probably the last thing those dying eyes had looked upon.

Death in horrible shape was all about me. I saw the work wrought by shrapnel, by gas, and the mangled red havoc of high explosive. I only seemed unreal, like one that walked in a nightmare. Here and there upon this sea of mud rose the twisted wreckage of aeroplanes, and from where I stood I counted five, but as I tramped on and on these five grew to nine. One of these lying upon my way I turned aside to glance at, and stared through a tangle of wires into a pallid thing that had been a face once comely and youthful; the leather jacket had been opened at the neck for the identity disc, as I suppose, and glancing lower, I saw that this leather jacket was discoloured, singed, burnt—and below this, a charred and unrecognisable mass.

Is there a man in the world to-day who, beholding such horrors, would not strive with all his strength to so order things that the hell of war should be made impossible henceforth? Therefore, I have recorded in some part what I have seen of war.

So now, all of you who read, I summon you in the name of our common humanity, let us be up and doing. Americans—Anglo-Saxons, let our common blood be a bond of brotherhood between us henceforth, a bond indissoluble. As you have now entered the war, as you are now our allies in deed as in spirit, let this alliance endure hereafter. Already there is talk of some such League, which, in its might and unity, shall secure humanity against any recurrence of the evils the world now groans under. Here is a noble purpose, and I conceive it the duty of each one of us, for the sake of those who shall come after, that we should do something to further that which was once looked upon as only an Utopian dream—the universal Brotherhood of Man.

"The flowers o' the forest are a' faded away."

Far and wide they lie, struck down in the flush of manhood, full of the joyous, unconquerable spirit of youth. Who knows what noble ambitions once were theirs, what splendid works they might not have wrought? Now they lie, each poor, shattered body a mass of loathsome corruption. Yet that diviner part, that no bullet may slay, no steel rend or mar, has surely entered into the fuller living, for Death is but the gateway into Life and infinite possibilities.

But, upon all who sit immune, upon all whom as yet this bitter war has left untouched, is the blood of these that died in the cause of humanity, the cause of Freedom for us and the generations to come, this blood is upon each one of us—consecrating us to the task they have died to achieve, and it is our solemn duty to see that the wounds they suffered, the deaths they died, have not been, and shall not be, in vain.

XII
FLYING MEN

A few short years ago flying was in its experimental stage; to-day, though man's conquest of the air is yet a dream unrealised, it has developed enormously and to an amazing degree; to-day, flying is one of the chief factors of this world war, both on sea and land. Upon the Western front alone there are thousands upon thousands of aeroplanes—monoplanes and biplanes—of hundreds of different makes and designs, of varying shapes and many sizes. I have seen giants armed with batteries of swivel guns and others mounting veritable cannon. Here are huge bomb-dropping machines with a vast wing spread; solid, steady-flying machines for photographic work, and the light, swift-climbing, double-gunned battle-planes, capable of mounting two thousand feet a minute and attaining a speed of two hundred kilometres. Of these last they are building scores a week at a certain factory I visited just outside Paris, and this factory is but one of many. But the men (or rather, youths) who fly these aerial marvels—it is of these rather than the machines that I would tell, since of the machines I can describe little even if I would; but I have watched them hovering unconcernedly (and quite contemptuous of the barking attention of "Archie") above white shrapnel bursts—fleecy, innocent-seeming puffs of smoke that go by the name of "woolly bears." I have seen them turn and hover and swoop, swift and graceful as great eagles. I have watched master pilots of both armies, English and French, perform soul-shaking gyrations high in air, feats quite impossible hitherto and never attempted until lately. There is now a course of aerial gymnastics which every flier must pass successfully before he may call himself a "chasing" pilot; and, from what I have observed, it would seem that to become a pilot one must be either all nerve or possess no nerve at all.

Conceive a biplane, thousands of feet aloft, suddenly flinging its nose up and beginning to climb vertically as if intending to loop the loop; conceive of its pausing suddenly and remaining, for perhaps a full minute, poised thus upon its tail—absolutely perpendicular. Then, the engines switched off, conceive of it falling helplessly, tail first, reversing suddenly and plunging earthwards, spinning giddily round and round very like the helpless flutter of a falling leaf. Then suddenly, the engine roars again, the twisting, fluttering, dead thing becomes instinct with life, rights itself majestically on flashing pinions, swoops down in swift and headlong course, and turning, mounts the wind and soars up and up as light, as graceful, as any bird.

Other nerve-shattering things they do, these soaring young demigods of the air, feats so marvellous to such earth-bound ones as myself—feats indeed so wildly daring it would seem no ordinary human could ever hope to attain unto. But in and around Paris and at the front, I have talked with, dined with, and known many of these bird-men, both English, French and American, and have generally found them very human indeed, often shy, generally simple and unaffected, and always modest of their achievements and full of admiration for seamen and soldiers, and heartily glad that their lives are not jeopardised aboard ships, or submarines, or in muddy trenches; which sentiment I have heard fervently expressed—not once, but many times. Surely the mentality of the flier is beyond poor ordinary understanding!

It was with some such thought in my mind that with my friend N., a well-known American correspondent, I visited one of our flying squadrons at the front. The day was dull and cloudy, and N., deep versed and experienced in flying and matters pertaining thereto, shook doubtful head.

"We shan't see much to-day," he opined, "low visibility—*plafond* only about a thousand!" Which cryptic sentence, by dint of pertinacious questioning, I found to mean that the clouds were about a thousand feet from earth and that it was misty. "*Plafond*", by the way, is aeronautic for cloud strata. Thus I stood with my gaze lifted heavenward until the Intelligence Officer joined us with a youthful flight-captain, who, having shaken hands, looked up also and stroked a small and very young moustache. And presently he spoke as nearly as I remember on this wise:

"About twelve hundred! Rather rotten weather for our business— expecting some new machines over, too."

"Has your squadron been out lately?" I enquired (I have the gift of enquiry largely developed).

"Rather! Lost four of our chaps yesterday—'Archie' got 'em. Rotten bad luck!"

"Are they—hurt?" I asked.

"Well, we know two are all right, and one we think is, but the other—rather a pal of mine—"

"Do you often lose fellows?"

"Off and on—you see, we're a fighting squadron—must take a bit of risk now and then—it's the game, y'know!"

He brought me where stood biplanes and monoplanes of all sizes and designs, and paused beside a two-seater, gunned fore and aft, and with ponderous, wide-flung wings.

"This," he explained, "is an old battle-plane, quite a veteran too—jolly old bus in its way, but too slow; it's a 'pusher', you see, and 'tractors' are all the go. We're having some over to-day—tophole machines." Here ensued much technical discussion between him and N. as to the relative merits of traction and propulsion.

"Have you had many air duels?" I enquired at last, as we wandered on through a maze of wheels and wings and propellers.

"Oh, yes, one or two," he admitted, "though nothing very much!" he hastened to add. "Some of our chaps are pretty hot stuff, though. There's B. now; B.'s got nine so far."

"An air fight must be rather terrible?" said I.

"Oh, I don't know!" he demurred. "Gets a bit lively sometimes. C., one of our chaps, had a near go coming home yesterday—attacked by five Boche machines, well over their own territory, of course. They swooped down on him out of a cloud. C. got one right away, but the others got him—nearly. They shot his gear all to pieces and put his bally gun out of commission—bullet clean through the tray. Rotten bad luck! So, being at their mercy, C. pretended they'd got him—did a turn-over and nose-dived through the clouds very nearly on two more Boche machines that were waiting for him. So, thinking it was all up with him, C. dived straight for the nearest, meaning to take a Boche down with him, but Hans didn't think that was playing the game, and promptly hooked it. The other fellow had been blazing away and was getting a new drum fixed, when he saw C. was on his tail making tremendous business with his useless gun, so Fritz immediately dived away out of range, and C. got home with about fifty bullet holes in his wings and his gun crocked, and—oh, here he is!"

Flight-Lieutenant C. appeared, rather younger than his Captain, a long, slender youth, with serious brow and thoughtful eyes, whom I forthwith questioned as diplomatically as might be.

"Oh, yes!" he answered, in response to my various queries, "it was exciting for a minute or so, but I expect the Captain has been pulling your leg no end. Yes, they smashed my gun. Yes, they hit pretty well everything except me and my mascot—they didn't get that, by good luck. No, I don't think a fellow would mind 'getting it' in the ordinary way—a bullet, say. But it's the damned petrol catching alight and burning one's legs." Here the speaker bent to survey his long legs with serious eyes. "Burning isn't a very nice finish somehow. They generally manage to chuck themselves out—when they can. Hello—here comes one of our new machines—engine sounds nice and smooth!" said he, cocking an ear. Sure enough, came a faint purr that grew to a hum, to an ever-loudening drone, and out from the clouds an aeroplane appeared, which, wheeling in graceful spirals, sank lower and lower, touched earth, rose, touched again, and so, engine roaring, slid smoothly toward us over the grass. Then appeared men in blue overalls, who seized the gleaming monster in unawed, accustomed hands, steadied it, swung it round, and halted it within speaking distance.

Hereupon its leather-clad pilot climbed stiffly out, vituperated the weather and lit a cigarette.

"How is she?" enquired the Captain.

"A lamb! A witch! Absolutely tophole when you get used to her." The tophole lamb and witch was a smallish biplane with no great wing spread, but powerfully engined, whose points N. explained to me as—her speed, her climbing angle, her wonderful stability, etc., while the Captain and Lieutenant hastened off to find the Major, who, appearing in due course, proved to be slender, merry-eyed and more youthful-looking than the Lieutenant. Indeed, so young seeming was he that upon better acquaintance I ventured to enquire his age, and he somewhat unwillingly owned to twenty-three.

"But," said he, "I'm afraid we can't show you very much, the weather's so perfectly rotten for flying."

"Oh, I don't know," said the Captain, glancing towards the witch-lamb, "I rather thought I'd like to try this new machine—if you don't mind, sir."

"Same here," murmured the Lieutenant.

"But you've never flown a Nieuport before, have you, eh?" enquired the Major.

"No, sir, but—"

"Nor you either, C.?"

"No, sir, still—"

"Then I'll try her myself," said the Major, regarding the witch-lamb joyous-eyed.

"But," demurred the Captain, "I was rather under the impression you'd never flown one either."

"I haven't—yet," laughed the Major, and hasted away for his coat and helmet.

"Can you beat that?" exclaimed the Lieutenant.

The Captain sighed and went to aid the Major into his leathern armour. Lightly and joyously the youthful Major climbed into the machine and sat awhile to examine and remark upon its unfamiliar features, while a sturdy mechanic stood at the propeller ready to start the engine.

"By the way," said he, turning to address me. "You're staying to luncheon, of course?"

"I'm afraid we can't," answered our Intelligence Officer.

"Oh, but you must—I've ordered soup! Right-oh!" he called to his mechanician; the engine hummed, thundered, and roaring, cast back upon us a very gale of wind; the witch-lamb moved, slid forward over the grass, and gathering speed, lifted six inches, a yard, ten yards—and was in flight.

"Can you beat that?" exclaimed the Captain enthusiastically, "lifted her clean away!"

"I rather fancy he's about as good as they're made!" observed the Lieutenant. Meanwhile, the witch-lamb soared up and up straight as an arrow; up she climbed, growing rapidly less until she was a gnat against a background of fleecy cloud and the roar of the engine had diminished to a whine; up and up until she was a speck—until the clouds had swallowed her altogether.

"Pity it isn't clear!" said the Captain. "I rather fancy you'd have seen some real flying. By the way, they're going to practise at the targets—might interest you. Care to see?"

The targets were about a yard square and, as I watched, an aeroplane rose, wheeling high above them. All at once the hum of the engine was lost in the sharp, fierce rattle of a machine gun; and ever as the biplane banked and wheeled the machine gun crackled. From every angle and from every point of the compass these bullets were aimed, and examining the targets afterwards I was amazed to see how many hits had been registered.

After this they brought me to the workshops where many mechanics were busied; they showed me, among other grim relics, C.'s broken machine gun and perforated cartridge tray. They told me many stories of daring deeds performed by other members of the squadron, but when I asked them to describe their own experiences, I found them diffident and monosyllabic.

"Hallo!" exclaimed C., as we stepped out into the air, "here comes the Major. He's in that cloud—know the sound of his engine." Sure enough, out from a low-lying cloud-bank he came, wheeling in short spirals, plunging earthward.

Down sank the aeroplane, the roaring engine fell silent, roared again, and she sped towards us, her wheels within a foot or so of earth. Finally they touched, the engine stopped and the witch-lamb pulled up within a few feet of us. Hereupon the Major waved a gauntleted hand to us.

"Must stop to lunch," he cried, "I've ordered soup, you know."

But this being impossible, we perforce said good-by to these warm-hearted, simple-souled fighting men, a truly regrettable farewell so far as I was concerned. They escorted us to the car, and there parted from us with many frank expressions of regard and stood side by side to watch us out of sight.

"Yesterday there was much aerial activity on our front.

"Depôts were successfully bombed and five enemy machines were forced to descend, three of them in flames. Four of ours did not return."

I shall never read these oft recurring lines in the communiqués without thinking of those three youthful figures, so full of life and the joy of life, who watched us depart that dull and cloudy morning.

Here is just one other story dealing with three seasoned air-fighters, veterans of many deadly combats high above the clouds, each of whom has more than one victory to his credit, and whose combined ages total up to sixty or thereabouts. We will call them X., Y. and Z. Now X. is an American, Y. is an Englishman, whose peach-like countenance yet bears the newly healed scar of a bullet wound, and Z. is an Afrikander. Here begins the story:

Upon a certain day of wind, rain and cloud, news came that the Boches were massing behind their lines for an attack, whereupon X., Y. and Z. were ordered to go up and verify this. Gaily enough they started despite unfavourable weather conditions. The clouds were low, very low, but they must fly lower, so, at an altitude varying from fifteen hundred to a bare thousand feet, they crossed the German lines, Y. and Z. flying wing and wing behind X.'s tail. All at once "Archie" spoke, a whole battery of anti-aircraft guns filled the air with smoke and whistling bullets—away went X.'s propeller and his machine was hurled upside down; immediately Y. and Z. rose. By marvellous pilotage X. managed to right his crippled machine and began, of course, to fall; promptly Y. and Z. descended. It is, I believe, an unwritten law in the Air Service never to desert a comrade until he is seen to be completely "done for"—hence Y. and Z.'s hawk-like swoop from the clouds to draw the fire of the battery from their stricken companion. Down they plunged through the battery smoke, firing their machine guns point-blank as they came; and so, wheeling in long spirals, their guns crackling viciously, they mounted again and soared cloudward together, but, there among the clouds and in comparative safety, Z. developed engine trouble. Their ruse had served, however, and X. had contrived to bring his shattered biplane to earth safely behind the British lines. Meanwhile Y. and Z. continued on toward their objective, but Z.'s engine trouble becoming chronic, he fell behind more and more, and finally, leaving Y. to carry on alone, was forced to turn back. And now it was that, in the mists ahead, he beheld another machine which, coming swiftly down upon him, proved to be a German, who, mounting above him, promptly opened fire. Z., struggling with his baulking engine, had his hands pretty full; moreover his opponent, owing to greater speed, could attack him from precisely what angle he chose. So they wheeled and flew, Z. endeavouring to bring his gun to bear, the German keeping skilfully out of range, now above him, now below, but ever and always behind. Thus the Boche flying on Z.'s tail had him at his mercy; a bullet ripped his sleeve, another smashed his speedometer, yet another broke his gauge—slowly and by degrees nearly all Z.'s gear is either smashed or carried away by bullets. All this time it is to be supposed that Z., thus defenceless, is wheeling and turning as well as his crippled condition will allow, endeavouring to get a shot at his elusive foe; but (as he told me) he felt it was his finish, so he determined if possible to ram his opponent and crash down with him through the clouds. Therefore, waiting until the Boche was aiming at him from directly below, he threw his machine into a sudden dive. Thus for one moment Z. had him in range, for a moment only, but the range was close and deadly, and Z. fired off half his tray as he swooped headlong down upon his astonished foe. All at once the German waved an arm and sagged over sideways, his great battle-plane wavering uncertainly, and, as it began to fall, Z. avoided the intended collision by inches. Down went the German machine, down and down, and, watching, Z. saw it plunge through the clouds wrapped in flame.

Then Z. turned and made for home as fast as his baulking engine would allow.

These are but two stories among dozens I have heard, yet these, I think, will suffice to show something of the spirit animating these young paladins. The Spirit of Youth is surely a godlike spirit, unconquerable, care-free, undying. It is a spirit to whom fear and defeat are things to smile and wonder at, to whom risks and dangers are joyous episodes, and Death himself, whose face their youthful eyes have so often looked into, a friend familiar by close acquaintanceship.

Upon a time I mentioned some such thought to an American aviator, who nodded youthful head and answered in this manner:

"The best fellows generally go first, and such a lot are gone now that there'll be a whole bunch of them waiting to say 'Hello, old sport!' so—what's it matter, anyway?"

XIII
YPRES

Much has been written concerning Ypres, but more, much more, remains to be written. Some day, in years to come, when the roar of guns has been long forgotten, and Time, that great and beneficent consoler, has dried the eyes that are now wet with the bitter tears of bereavement and comforted the agony of stricken hearts, at such a time some one will set down the story of Ypres in imperishable words; for round about this ancient town lie many of the best and bravest of Britain's heroic army. Thick, thick, they lie together, Englishman, Scot and Irishman, Australian, New Zealander, Canadian and Indian, linked close in the comradeship of death as they were in life; but the glory of their invincible courage, their noble self-sacrifice and endurance against overwhelming odds shall never fade. Surely, surely while English is spoken the story of "Wipers" will live on for ever and, through the coming years, will be an inspiration to those for whom these thousands went, cheering and undismayed, to meet and conquer Death.

Ypres, as all the world knows, forms a sharp salient in the British line, and is, therefore, open to attack on three sides; and on these three sides it has been furiously attacked over and over again, so very often that the mere repetition would grow wearisome. And these attacks were day-long, week- and sometimes month-long battles, but Britain's army stood firm.

In these bad, dark days, outnumbered and out-gunned, they never wavered. Raked by flanking fire they met and broke the charges of dense-packed foemen on their front; rank upon rank and elbow to elbow the Germans charged, their bayonets a sea of flashing steel, their thunderous shouts drowning the roar of guns, and rank on rank they reeled back from British steel and swinging rifle-butt, and German shouts died and were lost in British cheers.

So, day after day, week after week, month after month they endured still; swept by rifle and machine-gun fire, blown up by mines, buried alive by mortar bombs, their very trenches smitten flat by high explosives—yet they endured and held on. They died all day and every day, but their places were filled by men just as fiercely determined. And ever as the countless German batteries fell silent, their troops in dense grey waves hurled themselves upon shattered British trench and dugout, and found there wild men in tunics torn and bloody and mud-bespattered, who, shouting in fierce joy, leapt to meet them bayonet to bayonet. With clubbed rifle and darting steel they fought, these men of the Empire, heedless of wounds and death, smiting and cheering, thrusting and shouting, until those long, close-ranked columns broke, wavered and melted away. Then, panting, they cast themselves back into wrecked trench and blood-spattered shell hole while the enemy's guns roared and thundered anew, and waited patiently but yearningly for another chance to "really fight." So they held this deadly salient.

Days came and went, whole regiments were wiped out, but they held on. The noble town behind them crumbled into ruin beneath the shrieking avalanche of shells, but they held on. German and British dead lay thick from British parapet to Boche wire, and over this awful litter fresh attacks were launched daily, but still they held on, and would have held and will hold, until the crack of doom if need be—because Britain and the Empire expect it of them.

But to-day the dark and evil time is passed. To-day for every German shell that crashes into the salient, four British shells burst along the enemy's position, and it was with their thunder in my ears that I traversed that historic, battle-torn road which leads into Ypres, that road over which so many young and stalwart feet have tramped that never more may come marching back. And looking along this road, lined with scarred and broken trees, my friend N. took off his hat and I did the like.

"It's generally pretty lively here," said our Intelligence Officer, as I leaned forward to pass him the matches. "We're going to speed up a bit—road's a bit bumpy, so hold on." Guns were roaring near and far, and in the air above was the long, sighing drone of shells as we raced forward, bumping and swaying over the uneven surface faster and faster, until, skidding round a rather awkward corner, we saw before us a low-lying, jagged outline of broken walls, shattered towers and a tangle of broken roof-beams—all that remains of the famous old town of Ypres. And over this devastation shells moaned distressfully, and all around unseen guns barked and roared. So, amidst this pandemonium our car lurched into shattered "Wipers", past the dismantled water-tower, uprooted from its foundations and leaning at a more acute angle than will ever the celebrated tower of Pisa, past ugly heaps of brick and rubble—the ruins of once fair buildings, on and on until we pulled up suddenly before a huge something, shattered and formless, a long façade of broken arches and columns, great roof gone, mighty walls splintered, cracked and rent—all that "Kultur" has left of the ancient and once beautiful Cloth Hall.

"Roof's gone since I was here last," said the Intelligence Officer, "come this way. You'll see it better from over here." So we followed him and stood to look upon the indescribable ruin.

"There are no words to describe—that," said N. at last, gloomily.

"No," I answered. "Arras was bad enough, but this—!"

"Arras?" he repeated. "Arras is only a ruined town. Ypres is a rubbish dump. And its Cloth Hall is—a bad dream." And he turned away. Our Intelligence Officer led us over mounds of fallen masonry and débris of all sorts, and presently halted us amid a ruin of splintered columns, groined arch and massive walls, and pointed to a heap of rubbish he said was the altar.

"This is the Church St. Jean," he explained, "begun, I think, in the eleventh or twelfth century and completed somewhere about 1320—"

"And," said N., "finally finished and completely done for by 'Kultur' in the twentieth century, otherwise I guess it would have lasted until the 220th century—look at the thickness of the walls."

"And after all these years of civilisation," said I.

"Civilisation," he snorted, turning over a fragment of exquisitely carved moulding with the toe of his muddy boot, "civilisation has done a whole lot, don't forget—changed the system of plumbing and taught us how to make high explosives and poison gas."

Gloomily enough we wandered on together over rubbish piles and mountains of fallen brickwork, through shattered walls, past unlovely stumps of mason-work that had been stately tower or belfry once, beneath splintered arches that led but from one scene of ruin to another, and ever our gloom deepened, for it seemed that Ypres, the old Ypres, with all its monuments of mediæval splendour, its noble traditions of hard-won freedom, its beauty and glory, was passed away and gone for ever.

"I don't know how all this affects you," said N., his big chin jutted grimly, "but I hate it worse than a battlefield. Let's get on over to the Major's office."

We went by silent streets, empty except for a few soldierly figures in hard-worn khaki, desolate thoroughfares that led between piles and huge unsightly mounds of fallen masonry and shattered brickwork, fallen beams, broken rafters and twisted ironwork, across a desolate square shut in by the ruin of the great Cloth Hall and other once stately buildings, and so to a grim, battle-scarred edifice, its roof half blown away, its walls cracked and agape with ugly holes, its doorway reinforced by many sandbags cunningly disposed, through which we passed into the dingy office of the Town Major.

As we stood in that gloomy chamber, dim-lighted by a solitary oil lamp, floor and walls shook and quivered to the concussion of a shell—not very near, it is true, but quite near enough.

The Major was a big man, with a dreamy eye, a gentle voice and a passion for archæology. In his company I climbed to the top of a high building, whence he pointed out, through a convenient shell hole, where the old walls had stood long ago, where Vauban's star-shaped bastions were, and the general conformation of what had been present-day Ypres; but I saw only a dusty chaos of shattered arch and tower and walls, with huge, unsightly mounds of rubble and brick—a rubbish dump in very truth. Therefore I turned to the quiet-voiced Major and asked him of his experiences, whereupon he talked to me most interestingly and very learnedly of Roman tile, of mediæval rubble-work, of herringbone and Flemish bond. He assured me also that (*Deo volente*) he proposed to write a monograph on the various epochs of this wonderful old town's history as depicted by its various styles of mason-work and construction.

"I could show you a nearly perfect aqueduct if you have time," said he.

"I'm afraid we ought to be starting now," said the Intelligence Officer; "over eighty miles to do yet, you see, Major."

"Do you have many casualties still?" I enquired.

"Pretty well," he answered. "The mediæval wall was superimposed upon the Roman, you'll understand."

"And is it," said I as we walked on together, "is it always as noisy as this?"

"Oh, yes—especially when there's a 'Hate' on."

"Can you sleep?"

"Oh, yes, one gets used to anything, you know. Though, strangely enough, I was disturbed last night—two of my juniors had to camp over my head, their quarters were blown up rather yesterday afternoon, and believe me, the young beggars talked and chattered so that I couldn't get a wink of sleep—had to send and order them to shut up."

"You seem to have been getting it pretty hot since I was here last," said the Intelligence Officer, waving a hand round the crumbling ruin about us.

"Fairly so," nodded the Major.

"One would wonder the enemy wastes any more shells on Ypres," said I, "there's nothing left to destroy, is there?"

"Well, there's us, you know!" said the Major gently, "and then the Boche is rather a revengeful beggar anyhow—you see, he wasted quite a number of army corps trying to take Ypres. And he hasn't got it yet."

"Nor ever will," said I.

The Major smiled and held out his hand.

"It's a pity you hadn't time to see that aqueduct," he sighed. "However, I shall take some flashlight photos of it—if my luck holds. Good-by." So saying, he raised a hand to his weather-beaten trench cap and strode back into his dim-lit, dingy office.

The one-time glory of Ypres has vanished in ruin but thereby she has found a glory everlasting. For over the wreck of noble edifice and fallen tower is another glory that shall never fade but rather grow with coming years—an imperishable glory. As pilgrims sought it once to tread its quaint streets and behold its old-time beauty, so in days to come other pilgrims will come with reverent feet and with eyes that shall see in these shattered ruins a monument to the deathless valour of that brave host that met death unflinching and unafraid for the sake of a great ideal and the welfare of unborn generations.

And thus in her ruin Ypres has found the Glory Everlasting.

XIV
WHAT BRITAIN HAS DONE

The struggle of Democracy and Reason against Autocracy and Brute Force, on land and in the air, upon the sea and under the sea, is reaching its climax. With each succeeding month the ignoble foe has smirched himself with new atrocities which yet in the end bring their own terrible retribution.

Three of the bloodiest years in the world's history lie behind us; but these years of agony and self-sacrifice, of heroic achievements, of indomitable purpose and unswerving loyalty to an ideal, are surely three of the most tremendous in the annals of the British Empire.

I am to tell something of what Britain has accomplished during these awful three years, of the mighty changes she has wrought in this short time, of how, with her every thought and effort bent in the one direction, she has armed and equipped herself and many of her allies; of the armies she has raised, the vast sums she has expended and the munitions and armaments she has amassed.

To this end it is my privilege to lay before the reader certain facts and figures, so I propose to set them forth as clearly and briefly as may be, leaving them to speak for themselves.

For truly Britain has given and is giving much—her men and women, her money, her very self; the soul of Britain and her Empire is in this conflict, a soul that grows but the more steadfast and determined as the struggle waxes more deadly and grim. Faint hearts and fanatics there are, of course, who, regardless of the future, would fain make peace with the foe unbeaten, a foe lost to all shame and honourable dealing, but the heart of the Empire beats true to the old war-cry of "Freedom or Death." In proof of which, if proof be needed, let us to our figures and facts.

Take first her fighting men: in three short years her little army has grown until to-day seven million of her sons are under arms, and of these (most glorious fact!) nearly five million were *volunteers*. Surely since first this world was cursed by war, never did such a host march forth voluntarily to face its blasting horrors. They are fighting on many battle-fronts, these citizen-soldiers, in France, Macedonia, Mesopotamia, Palestine, Western Egypt and German East Africa, and behind them, here in the homeland, are the women, working as their men fight, with a grim and tireless determination. To-day the land hums with munition factories and huge works whose countless wheels whirr day and night, factories that have sprung up where the grass grew so lately. The terrible, yet glorious, days of Mons and the retreat, when her little army, out-gunned and out-manned, held up the rushing might of the German advance so long as life and ammunition lasted, that black time is past, for now in France and Flanders our countless guns crash in ceaseless concert, so that here in England one may hear their ominous muttering all day long and through the hush of night; and hearkening to that continuous stammering murmur one thanks God for the women of Britain.

Two years ago, in June, 1915, the Ministry of Munitions was formed under Mr. David Lloyd George; as to its achievements, here are figures which shall speak plainer than any words.

In the time of Mons the army was equipped and supplied by three Government factories and a very few auxiliary firms; to-day gigantic national factories, with miles of railroads to serve them, are in full swing, beside which, thousands of private factories are controlled by the Government. As a result the output of explosives in March, 1917, was over *four times* that of March, 1916, and *twenty-eight times* that of March, 1915, and so enormous has been the production of shells that in the first nine weeks of the summer offensive of 1917 the stock decreased by only seven per cent. despite the appalling quantity used.

The making of machine guns to-day as compared with 1915 has increased *twenty-fold*, while the supply of small-arm ammunition has become so abundant that the necessity for importation has ceased altogether. In one Government factory alone the making of rifles has increased *ten-fold*, and the employees at Woolwich Arsenal have increased from a little less than *eleven thousand* to nearly *seventy-four thousand*, of whom *twenty-five thousand* are women.

Production of steel, before the war, was roughly seven million tons; it is now ten million tons and still increasing, so much so that it is expected the pre-war output will be doubled by the end of 1918; while the cost of steel plates here is now less than half the cost in the U.S.A. Since May, 1917, the output of aeroplanes has been quadrupled and is rapidly increasing; an enormous programme of construction has been laid down and plans drawn up for its complete realisation.

With this vast increase in the production of munitions the cost of each article has been substantially reduced by systematic examination of actual cost, resulting in a saving of £43,000,000 over the previous year's prices.

Figures are a dry subject in themselves, and yet such figures as these are, I venture to think, of interest, among other reasons for the difficulty the human brain has to appreciate their full meaning. Thus: the number of articles handled weekly by the Stores Departments is several hundreds of thousands above fifty million: or again, I read that the munition workers themselves have contributed £40,187,381 towards various war loans. It is all very easy to write, but who can form any just idea of such uncountable numbers?

And now, writing of the sums of money Britain has already expended, I for one am immediately lost, out of my depth and plunged ten thousand fathoms deep, for now I come upon the following:

"The total national expenditure for the three years to August 4th, 1917, is approximately £5,150,000,000, of which £1,250,000,000 is already provided for by taxation and £1,171,000,000 has been lent to our colonies and allies, which may be regarded as an investment." Having written which I lay down my pen to think, and, giving it up, hasten to record the next fact.

"The normal pre-war taxation amounted to approximately £200,000,000, but for the current financial year (1917-1918) a revenue of £638,000,000 has been budgeted for, but this is expected to produce between £650,000,000 and £700,000,000." Now, remembering that the cost of necessaries has risen to an unprecedented extent, these figures of the extra taxation and the amounts raised by the various war loans speak louder and more eloquently than any words how manfully Britain has shouldered her burden and of her determination to see this great struggle through to the only possible conclusion—the end, for all time, of autocratic government.

I have before me so many documents and so much data bearing on this vast subject that I might set down very much more; I might descant on marvels of enterprise and organisation and of almost insuperable difficulties overcome. But, lest I weary the reader, and since I would have these lines read, I will hasten on to the last of my facts and figures.

As regards ships, Britain has already placed six hundred vessels at the disposal of France and four hundred have been lent to Italy, the combined tonnage of these thousand ships being estimated at two million.

Then, despite her drafts to Army and Navy she has still a million men employed in her coal mines and is supplying coal to Italy, France and Russia. Moreover, she is sending to France one quarter of her total production of steel, munitions of all kinds to Russia and guns and gunners to Italy.

As for her Navy—the German battle squadrons lie inactive, while in one single month the vessels of the British Navy steamed over one million miles; German trading ships have been swept from the seas and the U-boat menace is but a menace still. Meantime, British shipyards are busy night and day; a million tons of craft for the Navy alone were launched during the first year of the war, and the programme of new naval construction for 1917 runs into hundreds of thousands of tons. In peace time the building of new merchant ships was just under 2,000,000 tons yearly, and despite the shortage of labour and difficulty of obtaining materials, 1,100,000 tons will be built by the end of 1917, and 4,000,000 tons in 1918.

The British Mercantile Marine (to whom be all honour!) has transported during the war, the following:—

13,000,000 men,

25,000,000 tons of war material,

1,000,000 sick and wounded,

51,000,000 tons of coal and oil fuel,

2,000,000 horses and mules,

100,000,000 hundredweights of wheat,

7,000,000 tons of iron ore,

and, beyond this, has exported goods to the value of £500,000,000.

Here ends my list of figures and here this chapter should end also; but, before I close, I would give, very briefly and in plain language, three examples of the spirit animating this Empire that to-day is greater and more worthy by reason of these last three blood-smirched years.

No. I

There came from Australia at his own expense, one Thomas Harper, an old man of seventy-four, to help in a British munition factory. He laboured hard, doing the work of two men, and more than once fainted with fatigue, but refused to go home because he "couldn't rest while he thought his country needed shells."

No. II

There is a certain small fishing village whose men were nearly all employed in fishing for mines. But there dawned a black day when news came that forty of their number had perished together and in the same hour. Now surely one would think that this little village, plunged in grief for the loss of its young manhood, had done its duty to the uttermost for Britain and their fellows! But these heroic fisher-folk thought otherwise, for immediately fifty of the remaining seventy-five men (all over military age) volunteered and sailed away to fill the places of their dead sons and brothers.

No. III

Glancing idly through a local magazine some days since, my eye was arrested by this:

"In proud and loving memory of our loved and loving son ... who fell in France ... with his only brother, 'On Higher Service.' There is no death."

Thus then I conclude my list of facts and figures, a record of achievement such as this world has never known before, a record to be proud of, because it is the outward and visible sign of a people strong, virile, abounding in energy, but above all, a people clean of soul to whom Right and Justice are worth fighting for, suffering for, labouring for. It is the sign of a people which is willing to endure much for its ideals that the world may be a better world, wherein those who shall come hereafter may reap, in peace and contentment, the harvest this generation has sowed in sorrow, anguish and great travail.

THE END

FOOTNOTE

[1] Deleted by censor. J. F.